Cultural Institute

THE ROYAL COURT THEATRE PRESENTS

Poet in da Corner

by Debris Stevenson
Feat. Jammz

Poet in da Corner is part of Represent, a series of artworks inspired by the Representation of the People Act 1918.

Poet in da Corner was co-commissioned by 14-18 NOW and the Royal Court Theatre, supported by Jerwood Charitable Foundation, in association with Nottingham Playhouse and Leicester Curve.

Poet in da Corner was first performed at the Royal Court Jerwood Theatre Downstairs, Sloane Square, on Friday 21 September 2018.

Poet in da Corner

by Debris Stevenson
Feat. Jammz

CAST (in alphabetical order)

Tony+ **Kirubel Belay**
Mum+ **Cassie Clare**
SS Vyper **Jammz**
Debris **Debris Stevenson**

Director **Ola Ince**
Music Director/Lead Composer **Michael 'Mikey J' Asante**
Designer **Jacob Hughes**
Lighting Designer **Max Narula**
Choreographer **Aaron Sillis**
Assistant Director **Milli Bhatia**
Assistant Choreographer **Shanika Wallace**
Vocal Coach **Hazel Holder**
Krump Consultant **Dominant**
Producer **Erica Campayne**
Casting Director **Arthur Carrington**
Production Manager **Marty Moore**
Costume Supervisor **Lucy Walshaw**
Stage Manager **Nic Donithorn**
Deputy Stage Manager **Osnat Koblenz**
Set built by **The Next Stage**

Special thanks to Dizzee Rascal and Nick Cage.

Poet in da Corner
by Debris Stevenson
Feat. Jammz

Debris Stevenson (Writer/Performer)

Dyslexic-Writer, Grime Poet, Working-Class Academic, Pansexual Ex-Mormon and Bashment Dancing Social Activist from the seam between East London and Essex: it's not simple.

Debris Stevenson has no choice but to explore the intersectional, unexpected and unjust – it's not just who she is, it's her responsibility in a world that all too often summerises us into a caption.

At secondary school 2002 – 2008 Debris was educated through the evolution of Grime, finding poetry in the mouths of the teenagers around her. Nurtured by the Roundhouse, Debris was then followed by Channel 4 for a year (Yeardot), published by organisations such as Louis Vuitton, Oxford University, BBC Radio 4 and Flipped Eye with her debut pamphlet, Pigeon Party.

A social carrier pigeon, Debris has performed, written and taught poetry in over 20 countries and 10 American States. Her passion for nurturing and educating poetic communities started with The Mouthy Poets, teaching young people creative writing, performance and event coordination as emotional, professional and creative life skills.

Debris has since been granted over £250,000 by Arts Council England to develop young talent. She can also often be found dancing sober to Grime, Soca, Afrobeats and Dancehall for organisations such as The Heatwave and Red Bull Music Academy.

Michael 'Mikey J' Asante
(Music Director/Lead Composer)

Michael is a producer, composer, singer, dancer and DJ who is at the forefront of the UK urban music scene. Co-Founder & Co-Artistic Director of Boy Blue, who are an Associate Artist at the Barbican, he is a leading UK producer of live events.

Recent releases include George the Poet's Wotless with production and musical direction for George's sold-out Search Party tour, and engineering and production on Kano's critically acclaimed album Made In The Manor (Mercury Prize and BRIT nominated, and winner of the MOBO Best Album Award) with whom Michael has collaborated extensively on the albums Home Sweet Home, London Town and 140 Grime Street. Mikey is currently collaborating with the new Sony/Plan B signing Ryan De La Cruz.

Past production credits include Delilah's Inside My Love (From The Roots Up), Raleigh Ritchie's Stay Inside, Mikey J and the female All-stars, Estelle's Back to Love remix and Mz Brat's Get Dark. Michael has produced music for television, theatre and film including Boy Blue's Olivier Award nominated production Blak Whyte Gray, The Five & the Prophecy of Prana, Olivier Award winner Pied Piper: A Hip-Hop Dance Revolution, Touch and Legacy as well as the UK box office hits Street Dance 3D and All Stars.

In 2012, Michael worked closely with Kenrick 'H2O' Sandy, director Danny Boyle and musical directors Underworld, creating musical compositions for the Frankie and June say thanks Tim... section of London 2012 Olympic Games Opening Ceremony.

Kirubel Belay (Performer)

Music videos include: Like Sugar (Chaka Khan); Back for More (Example); Needing U (Desta French); Go Low (Jelani Blackman); Only (DJ Snake); What Is a Man? (ID Magazine).

Concerts & live events include: Peter Andre (UK Tour); Leona Lewis (Glassheart Tour); Kanye West (Brit Awards); Leah McFall (The Voice UK); Diversity Live (ITV); Michael Jackson (MTV); Omarion (KOKO Camden); Paloma Faith (Diageo Anniversary, Battersea Power Station).

As choreographer, music videos include: Moving Too Fast (Kyle Lettman ft. Scorcher).

Concert & live events include: Klickz Entertainment at Victoria & Albert Museum (Zibrant Events).

Milli Bhatia (Assistant Director)

As assistant director, for the Royal Court: One For Sorrow, Instructions for Correct Assembly, Girls & Boys.

As director, other theatre includes: Dismantle This Room, The Hijabi Monologues, My White Best Friend/This Bitter Earth [part of Black Lives Black Words] (Bush); I Have AIDS [Jerwood Assistant Director Programme] (Young Vic); Rats (Duffield Studio, National); EmpowerHouse (Theatre Royal, Stratford East); No Cowboys Only Indians (Courtyard).

As associate director, other theatre includes: What If Women Ruled the World? (Manchester International Festival).

As assistant director, other theatre includes: Lions & Tigers (Sam Wanamaker Playhouse);

Cell Mates, Filthy Business, Luna Gale (Hampstead); The Quiet House (& Park), The Government Inspector (& tour), What Shadows (Birmingham Rep).

Milli is Trainee Director at the Royal Court. She is an Associate Artist at the Bush Theatre and a Creative Associate at the Gate Theatre.

Erica Campayne (Producer)

Theatre includes: **Minefield, UpLIFTers, Kamyon, The Children's Choice Awards, The Hamilton Complex, Next Day, Cinema Imaginaire, Michael Essien I Want to Play As You, Deblozay, Turfed, 100% London, Ganesh Versus the Third Reich, The Dark Side of Love, Unfinished Dream, Home Sweet Home, FML, Haircuts by Children, Gloves On, Food Court (LIFT); All the President's Men, In Touch, The Jungle (National).**

Dance includes: **Political Mother: Derry~Londonderry (LIFT/Hofesh Shechter Company).**

Erica is a trustee of Bernie Grant Arts Centre. Her blog Kwame's Bookshelf reviews and promotes children's books which feature lead characters from diverse ethnicities.

Cassie Clare (Performer)

Theatre includes: **An Octoroon (National/Orange Tree); Little Shop of Horrors (UK tour); Oliver (Curve, Leicester); CATS (West End/European tour); Nights (White Bear).**

Television includes: **Delicious, The Bisexual, Endeavour, Maigret, The Coroner.**

Film includes: **Aladdin, Mamma Mia! Here We Go Again, Death Race 4, What Happened to Monday, Beauty & the Beast.**

Jacob Hughes (Designer)

Theatre includes: **The Rise & Fall of Little Voice (Park); Broad Shadow, KLT (National); Start Swimming (Young Vic); Twilight: Los Angeles 1992 (Gate); Treasure Island (Watford Palace); Napoleon Blown Apart (Arcola); The Aeneid (Oxford Playhouse); Sexual Perversity in Chicago (Sherman/National tour); Mr Swallow – Houdini [costume] (Soho); Mojo, She Stoops to Conquer, The Island, The Dark Things, Strawberry & Chocolate, The Prince of Homburg, Mydidae, Lift Off, Boom, Copenhagen (LAMDA); Titus Andronicus (Bedlam/Theatre Royal, York); Not the Messiah (Theatre503/West End); King Lear (Bute); Faith Hope & Humanity, Saved (RWCMD); War Whores (Courtyard); The Domino Heart, Valley of Song (Finborough); The Bald Prima Donna, The Blind, The Intruder (Old Red Lion); Merlin Unchained, Fridays Are Vermillion (Aberystwyth Arts Centre).**

Opera includes: **Un Ballo in Maschera, Il Trovatore (Winslow Hall).**

Event design includes: **The World Music Expo (Cardiff Motorpoint Arena); NT Up Next Gala [co-designer] (National).**

As associate/assistant designer, theatre includes: **Dusty the Musical (West End/UK tour); The Red Barn, Love, Sunset at the Villa Thalia, The Suicide (National); Manon Lescaut (ROH); The King's Speech (St Pauli, Hamburg); Le Nozze Di Figgaro (Haus für Mozart, Salzburg).**

Awards include: **Max Rayne Design Bursary Award for Emerging Artists.**

Ola Ince (Director)

For the Royal Court: **White Sky (& RWCMD/Gate).**

Other theatre includes: **Twilight: Los Angeles 1992 (Gate); Start Swimming (& Summerhall), Dutchman, One Million Tiny Plays About Britain (Young Vic); Broad Shadow, Access Denied, Cutting It (National); Rachel, The Soft of Her Palm (Finborough); Pets Corner (Arcola); Games (Pleasance).**

As associate director, theatre includes: **Tina: The Musical (West End); Tipping the Velvet (& Royal Lyceum, Edinburgh), Bugsy Malone (Lyric, Hammersmith); Fog (UK tour).**
As assistant director, theatre includes: **Shakespeare Trilogy (Donmar/St. Ann's Warehouse, New York); Ma Rainey's Black Bottom, Dara, A Taste of Honey (National); Porgy & Bess (Regent's Park Open Air); Josephine & I (Bush); Wild Swans, Disco Pigs, Electra (Young Vic); Fanta Orange, Blue Serge (Finborough); Secret Thoughts, The Demolition Man (Octagon, Bolton).**

Awards include: **Genesis Future Director Award.**

Ola has been Resident Assistant Director and Senior Reader at the Finborough Theatre, and was recipient of the Rose Bruford Directing Bursary and the Boris Karloff Bursary. In 2015 Ola became a BBC Performing Arts Fellow and Resident Associate Director at the Lyric Theatre, Hammersmith. She is currently an Associate Director at the Royal Court and Artistic Associate at the Lyric, Hammersmith and Theatre Royal Stratford East.

Jammz (Feature Writer/Performer)

Jammz came up studying Grime and in 2018 finds himself at the forefront of it. Born and bred in East London, Jammz started to make a name for himself on London's radio circuit in 2014 and 2015 appearing regularly on Rinse FM, Radar Radio, NTS, Mode FM and BBC 1xtra, teaming up with established DJs like Slimzee, Spooky, Bok Bok and Spyro as well as newcomers like Moleskin and Finn. His free EP Hit Then Run became a cult classic: the title track was playlisted on BBC 1Xtra and Noisey's

#3 Grime track of 2015, and the remix was Sian Anderson's #1 Remix of the Week six weeks on the spin.

Subsequent singles Final Warning and London Living further established Jammz as one of Grime's best new hit-makers, while his live reputation is also quickly on the rise: he's been booked for Glastonbury, Eskimo Dance, Outlook, Night Slugs and Bestival, has headlined FWD>> and in March 2016 was the support act on Kano's UK tour. Jammz has been supported heavily by Fader, Noisey, FACT, GQ, Mixmag, SBTV, MTV and more, and featured on the front cover of the Observer Music's British MCs special.

Jammz's first release of 2016, Mr. Wait (a collaboration with Trends & Mr. Dubz) was recently featured on Channel 4 and picked as one of Sleaford Mods' favourite tracks. He followed that with the acclaimed Underdog Season Vol. 1 mixtape (with Jack Dat), a self-released instrumental 12" (which sold out in four days) and a collaboration with Dread D on Local Action, 10 Missed Calls. 2017 saw the release of the DJ Q produced smash, Who's that girl? featuring Aleisha Lee, which received constant airplay across all mainstream stations including BBC Radio 1Xtra, Rinse FM and more. Jammz recently dropped Get What I Mean? through Annie Mac's Free Music Mondays and has EPs on I Am Grime and Local Action scheduled after the summer.

Max Narula (Lighting Designer)

For the Royal Court: **Birthday [as associate]**.

Other theatre includes: **Pop – Circus Festival (Roundhouse); Napoli Millonaria (Milton Court, Barbican); The Hour We Knew Nothing of Each Other (Silk Street, Barbican); Hamlet (Milton Court, Barbican); See What I See (St Clements Hospital)**.

As associate lighting designer, other theatre includes: **Strictly Ballroom (Princess of Wales, Toronto/ Playhouse, Leeds); The Girls Musical (& Lowry/ Grand, Leeds), Close to You (& Menier), Strangers on a Train, Big Fish, The Birthday Party, Tina! The Musical, Venus in Fur, Ink, The Wind in the Willows, Stepping Out (West End); Destiny (MGM Macau); Tell Me On a Sunday (Majestic, Shanghai); Elf the Musical (& West End), Big the Musical (Theatre Royal, Plymouth/ Bord Gáis Energy, Dublin); Mickey & the Magician (Disney Imagineering); Single Spies (Chichester); Full Monty, Rebecca (UK tour); Marco Polo (Guangzhou Opera House/Tianqiao Performing Arts Center, Beijing); Future Conditional (Old Vic); Closer (Donmar); Soho Cinders (Soho); The Soldier's Tale (Metropolitan, Tokyo); Josephine & I (Bush); Oil (Almeida)**.

As associate lighting designer, dance includes: **Les Enfants Terribles (Royal Ballet/ Barbican); Whelan/ Watson: Stories (ROH/City Center, NYC)**.

Max was awarded the Gold Medal Award from the Guildhall School of Music and Drama.

Aaron Sillis (Choreographer)

Theatre includes: **FKA twigs: Soundtrack 7 (Manchester International Festival)**.

Concert & live events include: **Years & Years (Palo Santo World Tour/Radio One's Biggest Weekend/ The Graham Norton Show); Laura Mvula (Glastonbury/Somerset House/The Graham Norton Show); FKA twigs (Roundhouse/ Brooklyn's Hangar/FYF LA/BRITS Are Coming/ Glastonbury/MOBO Awards); Kylie Minogue (Royal Variety Show/Strictly Come Dancing/The X Factor)**.

As director, music videos include: **Goldchains (Tyde Levi)**.

Awards include: **The Times Breakthrough Award (Dance), Southbank Sky Arts Awards**.

Aaron has choreographed music videos for Anna Calvi, Elton John, FKA twigs, Imagine Dragons, Jungle, Kylie Minogue, The Last Shadow Puppets, M.I.A & Sir Paul McCartney. He has also choreographed advertising campaigns for brands including Calvin Klein, Chanel, Hermés, Issey Miyake, Lacoste, Nike & Vogue.

Shanika Wallace
(Assistant Choreographer)

As choreographer, music videos include: **Ring Ring (Jax Jones X Mabel)**.

As director/choreographer, film includes: **London Girls, London Tracks**.

As assistant choreographer, music videos include: **Needing U, Mention (Desta French); Do It (Rae Morris)**.

As assistant choreographer, concert & live events include: **Years & Years (Palo Santo World Tour)**.

THE ROYAL COURT THEATRE

The Royal Court Theatre is the writers' theatre. It is a leading force in world theatre for energetically cultivating writers – undiscovered, emerging and established.

Through the writers, the Royal Court is at the forefront of creating restless, alert, provocative theatre about now. We open our doors to the unheard voices and free thinkers that, through their writing, change our way of seeing.

Over 120,000 people visit the Royal Court in Sloane Square, London, each year and many thousands more see our work elsewhere through transfers to the West End and New York, UK and international tours, digital platforms, our residencies across London, and our site-specific work. Through all our work we strive to inspire audiences and influence future writers with radical thinking and provocative discussion.

The Royal Court's extensive development activity encompasses a diverse range of writers and artists and includes an ongoing programme of writers' attachments, readings, workshops and playwriting groups. Twenty years of the International Department's pioneering work around the world means the Royal Court has relationships with writers on every continent.

Within the past sixty years, John Osborne, Samuel Beckett, Arnold Wesker, Ann Jellicoe, Howard Brenton and David Hare have started their careers at the Court.
Many others including Caryl Churchill, Athol Fugard, Mark Ravenhill, Simon Stephens, debbie tucker green, Sarah Kane – and, more recently, Lucy Kirkwood, Nick Payne, Penelope Skinner and Alistair McDowall – have followed.

The Royal Court has produced many iconic plays from Lucy Kirkwood's **The Children** to Jez Butterworth's **Jerusalem** and Martin McDonagh's **Hangmen**.

Royal Court plays from every decade are now performed on stage and taught in classrooms and universities across the globe.

It is because of this commitment to the writer that we believe there is no more important theatre in the world than the Royal Court.

Supported using public funding by
ARTS COUNCIL ENGLAND

In 1918, the Representation of the People Act granted the first women in this country the right to vote. After years of war, when women's work on the home front had been so essential, attitudes had shifted, influencing the government's decision to give women the vote for the first time.

This landmark Act of Parliament did not give women equal rights to men. While it granted the vote to all men over the age of 21, women had to be over 30 years old and on the property register – which excluded roughly one-third of women in the country. A further Act of Parliament in November 1918 gave women the right to stand for election as MPs, but it would be a further 10 years before women achieved equal franchise with men.

Poet in da Corner is one of three works that make up *Represent*, a 2018 series inspired both by the centenary of Votes for Women and by the inequalities it maintained in society. The series invites three radical young female artists to explore their experiences of democracy, equality and inclusion in contemporary Britain.

Had she been born 100 years earlier, Debris Stevenson would have been among the one-third of British women too young to benefit from the Representation of the People Act 1918. Her powerful work explores her fight to find her own voice and make it heard in a society that, even today, is not good at listening to young women.

Our great thanks go to our partners for their work on bringing *Poet in da Corner* to the stage to Vicky Featherstone, Lucy Davies, Erica Campayne and all at the Royal Court Theatre; to Jerwood Charitable Foundation, whose support and partnership has made *Represent* possible; and, most of all, to Debris and her creative team.

Represent is part of 14-18 NOW, the UK's five-year arts programme for the First World War centenary, and also features two other new works by young British artists: Selina Thompson's *Sortition*, a participatory performance piece; and Rachel Maclean's film *Make Me Up*. All three works speak vividly, in very different ways, of how the fight for women's rights and equality continues today.

Jenny Waldman
Director, 14-18 NOW

Supported using public funding by

  Department for Digital, Culture Media & Sport

LOTTERY FUNDED

COMING UP AT THE ROYAL COURT

24 – 27 Oct

Trying It On
Written and performed by David Edgar

Presented by Warwick Arts Centre and China Plate.

25 Oct – 24 Nov

ear for eye
By debbie tucker green

Produced in association with Barbara Broccoli.

31 Oct – 17 Nov

Still No Idea
Lisa Hammond and Rachael Spence

with Improbable and the Royal Court Theatre.

28 Nov – 12 Jan

Hole
By Ellie Kendrick

Hole is part of the Royal Court's Jerwood New Playwrights programme, supported by Jerwood Charitable Foundation.

6 Dec – 26 Jan

The Cane
By Mark Ravenhill

14 Feb – 16 Mar

Cyprus Avenue
By David Ireland

A Royal Court Theatre and Abbey Theatre production. The original production at the Royal Court in 2016 was supported by Cockayne Grants for the Arts, a donor-advised fund of the London Community Foundation.

Tickets from £12

royalcourttheatre.com

Sloane Square London, SW1W 8AS   ⊖ Sloane Square
⇌ Victoria Station   🐦 royalcourt   🇫 royalcourttheatre

 Supported using public funding by **ARTS COUNCIL ENGLAND**

 JERWOOD CHARITABLE FOUNDATION

ROYAL COURT SUPPORTERS

The Royal Court is a registered charity and not-for-profit company. We need to raise £1.5 million every year in addition to our core grant from the Arts Council and our ticket income to achieve what we do.

We have significant and longstanding relationships with many generous organisations and individuals who provide vital support. Royal Court supporters enable us to remain the writers' theatre, find stories from everywhere and create theatre for everyone.

We can't do it without you.

PUBLIC FUNDING

Arts Council England, London
British Council

TRUSTS & FOUNDATIONS

The Backstage Trust
The Bryan Adams Charitable Trust
The Austin & Hope Pilkington Trust
Martin Bowley Charitable Trust
Gerald Chapman Fund
CHK Charities
The City Bridge Trust
The Clifford Chance Foundation
Cockayne - Grants for the Arts
The Ernest Cook Trust
The Nöel Coward Foundation
Cowley Charitable Trust
The Eranda Rothschild Foundation
Lady Antonia Fraser for The Pinter Commission
Genesis Foundation
The Golden Bottle Trust
The Haberdashers' Company
The Paul Hamlyn Foundation
Roderick & Elizabeth Jack
Jerwood Charitable Foundation
The Mackintosh Foundation
The Andrew Lloyd Webber Foundation
The London Community Foundation

John Lyon's Charity
Clare McIntyre's Bursary
Old Possum's Practical Trust
The Andrew W. Mellon Foundation
The David & Elaine Potter Foundation
The Richard Radcliffe Charitable Trust
Rose Foundation
Royal Victoria Hall Foundation
The Sackler Trust
The Sobell Foundation
Span Trust
John Thaw Foundation
Unity Theatre Trust
The Wellcome Trust
The Garfield Weston Foundation

CORPORATE SPONSORS

Aqua Financial Solutions Ltd
Cadogan Estates
Colbert
Edwardian Hotels, London
Fever-Tree
Gedye & Sons
Kirkland & Ellis International LLP
Kudos
MAC
Room One
Sister Pictures
Sky Drama

CORPORATE MEMBERS

Gold
Weil, Gotshal & Manges LLP

Silver
Auerbach & Steele Opticians
Bloomberg
CNC – Communications & Network Consulting
Cream
Left Bank Pictures
Rockspring Property Investment Managers
Tetragon Financial Group

For more information or to become a foundation or business supporter contact Camilla Start: camillastart@royalcourttheatre.com/020 7565 5064.

Supported using public funding by
**ARTS COUNCIL
ENGLAND**

INDIVIDUAL SUPPORTERS

Artistic Director's Circle
Eric Abraham
Carolyn Bennett
Samantha & Richard
  Campbell-Breeden
Cas Donald
Jane Featherstone
Lydia & Manfred Gorvy
Jean & David Grier
Charles Holloway
Luke Johnson
Jack & Linda Keenan
Mandeep & Sarah Manku
Anatol Orient
NoraLee & Jon Sedmak
Deborah Shaw
  & Stephen Marquardt
Matthew & Sian Westerman
Mahdi Yahya

Writers' Circle
Chris & Alison Cabot
Jordan Cook & John Burbank
Scott M. Delman
Virginia Finegold
Michelle & Jan Hagemeier
Chris Hogbin
Mark Kelly & Margaret
  McDonald Kelly
Nicola Kerr
Emma O'Donoghue
Tracy Phillips
Suzanne Pirret
Theo & Barbara Priovolos
Sir Paul & Lady Ruddock
Carol Sellars
Maria Sukkar
Jan & Michael Topham
Maureen & Tony Wheeler
Anonymous

Directors' Circle
Mrs Asli Arah
Dr Kate Best
Katie Bradford
Piers Butler
Sir Trevor & Lady Chinn
Emma & Phil Coffer
Joachim Fleury
Piers & Melanie Gibson
Louis Greig
David & Claudia Harding
Dr Timothy Hyde
Roderick & Elizabeth Jack
Mrs Joan Kingsley
Victoria Leggett
Emma Marsh
Rachel Mason
Andrew & Ariana Rodger
Simon Tuttle
Anonymous

Platinum Members
Simon A Aldridge
Moira Andreae
Nick Archdale
Clive & Helena Butler
Gavin & Lesley Casey
Sarah & Philippe Chappatte
Andrea & Anthony Coombs
Clyde Cooper
Victoria Corcoran
Mrs Lara Cross
Andrew & Amanda Cryer
Shane & Catherine Cullinane
Matthew Dean
Sarah Denning
Cherry & Rob Dickins
The Drabble Family
Denise & Randolph Dumas
Robyn Durie
Mark & Sarah Evans
Sally & Giles Everist
Celeste Fenichel
Emily Fletcher
The Edwin Fox Foundation
Dominic & Claire Freemantle
Beverley Gee
Paul & Kay Goswell
Nick & Julie Gould
The Richard Grand Foundation
Jill Hackel & Andrzej Zarzycki
Carol Hall
Sam & Caroline Haubold
Mr & Mrs Gordon Holmes
Damien Hyland
Amanda & Chris Jennings
Ralph Kanter
Jim & Wendy Karp
David P Kaskel
  & Christopher A Teano
Vincent & Amanda Keaveny
Peter & Maria Kellner
Mr & Mrs Pawel Kisielewski
Rosemary Leith
Mark & Sophie Lewisohn
Kathryn Ludlow
The Maplescombe Trust
Christopher Marek
  Rencki
Frederic Marguerre
Mrs Janet Martin
Andrew McIver
David & Elizabeth Miles
Jameson & Lauren Miller
David Mills
Barbara Minto
M.E. Murphy Altschuler
Peter & Maggie Murray-Smith
Sarah Muscat
Liv Nilssen
Georgia Oetker
Crispin Osborne
Andrea & Hilary Ponti
Greg & Karen Reid
Nick & Annie Reid

Paul & Gill Robinson
Corinne Rooney
William & Hilary Russell
Sally & Anthony Salz
Anita Scott
Bhags Sharma
Dr. Wendy Sigle
Andy Simpkin
Paul & Rita Skinner
Brian Smith
John Soler & Meg Morrison
Kim Taylor-Smith
Mrs Caroline Thomas
Alex Timken
The Ulrich Family
Monica B Voldstad
Arrelle & François Von Hurter
Mr N C Wiggins
Anne-Marie Williams
Sir Robert & Lady Wilson
Anonymous

With thanks to our Friends, Silver and Gold Members whose support we greatly appreciate.

DEVELOPMENT COUNCIL

Piers Butler
Chris Cabot
Cas Donald
Sally Everist
Celeste Fenichel
Tim Hincks
Emma Marsh
Anatol Orient
Andrew Rodger
Sian Westerman

Our Supporters contribute to all aspects of the Royal Court's work including: productions, commissions, writers' groups, International, Young Court, creative posts, the Trainee scheme and access initiatives as well as providing in-kind support.

For more information or to become a Supporter please contact Charlotte Cole: charlottecole@ royalcourttheatre. com/020 7565 5049.

"There are no spaces, no rooms in my opinion, with a greater legacy of fearlessness, truth and clarity than this space."

Simon Stephens, Associate Playwright

The Royal Court invests in the future of the theatre, offering writers the support, time and resources to find their voices and tell their stories, asking the big questions and responding to the issues of the moment.

As a registered charity, the Royal Court needs to raise at least £1.5 million every year in addition to our Arts Council funding and ticket income, to keep seeking out, developing and nurturing new voices. Please join us by donating today.

You can donate online at **royalcourttheatre.com/donate** or via our **donation box in the Bar & Kitchen.**

We can't do it without you.

To find out more about the different ways in which you can be involved please contact Charlotte Cole on 020 7565 5049 / charlottecole@royalcourttheatre.com

Support the Court

The English Stage Company at the Royal Court Theatre is a registered charity (No. 231242).

POET IN DA CORNER

Debris Stevenson feat. Jammz

POET IN DA CORNER

OBERON BOOKS
LONDON

WWW.OBERONBOOKS.COM

First published in 2018 by Oberon Books Ltd
521 Caledonian Road, London N7 9RH
Tel: +44 (0) 20 7607 3637 / Fax: +44 (0) 20 7607 3629
e-mail: info@oberonbooks.com
www.oberonbooks.com

PB ISBN: 9781786826732
E ISBN: 9781786826749

Cover image: Benji Reid

Printed and bound by 4EDGE Limited, Hockley, Essex, UK.
eBook conversion by Lapiz Digital Services, India.

Visit www.oberonbooks.com to read more about all our books and to buy them. You
will also find features, author interviews and news of any author events, and you can
sign up for e-newsletters so that you're always first to hear about our new releases.

Printed on FSC accredited paper

10 9 8 7 6 5 4 3 2 1

"And the skies are all empty
cause the stars are on the ground"

from 'Get By' by Dizzee Rascal

This show would not have been possible without the UK grime scene (many, but not all, are mentioned in the show) and the community of people I've had around me from a young age – not to mention the 3-4 years *Poet in da Corner* developed as an idea before I had the honor of piecing it together with my amazing team at The Royal Court. I would not exist without these people, they are miraculous in a plethora of ways, and I need to thank them:

For having bars so good I memorized them all: Python.

For guiding me: Jacob Sam-La Rose and Charlie Dark.

For developing the idea and script: Suba Das, Giles Croft, Gareth Morgan, Nathan Powell, Hannah Silva, Community Recording Studios, Trevor Rose, Sabrina Mahfouz, every Mouthy Poet and Benji Reid.

For making me feel comfortable in the booth, my skin and on a track: Shemzy and Nick Stez.

For documenting the process through imagery and film: Tom Morley, Jamal Sterret, Ryan Hawkins, Saira Awan, Romany-Francesca Mukoro and Alice Russell.

For loving grime as much as me and writing about it: Kayo Chingonyi, Caleb Femi, Raphael Blake and Bridie Squires.

For writing and spitting bars alongside me: Eklipse, Tyreece, Omari, Nat, Adee, Relic, 2Tone, Jah Diggah, Asherr X and True Mendous.

For making amazing beats for me: Rapsz Katai, The Last Skeptikk, Bamz, Yazzuss and Lewis Fromberg.

For being the most open, loving, exciting DJs I've ever worked with: Premz, AG and Fever.

For not disowning me for writing about our lives: Gary, Richard, Mum and Dad.

And finally, Erica Campayne for being the most humble, heart-warming producing ninja I've ever worked with, Gill for protecting my space to write, Jammz for working with me on the script (writing SS Vyper and the DJ), Mikey J for not just making the music but teaching me about the origins of grime, Ola for bringing this huge community of people together so succinctly and Vicky, Chris and Hamish at the Royal Court for believing me more than I believed in myself. You all went above and beyond your job to make this a brilliant and important piece of work.

Dizzee was the foundation but you are the stars upon it.

Debris x

To listen to the tracks from *Poet in da Corner* visit
https://soundcloud.com/royal-court-theatre

Show starts, present day, DEBRIS is 28.

Introduction

HYPE: Okaayy, before we get things started I need to do a
mic check with you all. You're going to hear some poetry
tonight, but you're also going to hear some grime. In case
you don't know, Royal Court, this is what

Grime is…

*DJ plays series of snippets of different MCs explaining what grime
is in a variety of songs.*

How to respond to poetry and grime isn't obvious to
everyone… So let's start with poetry for a sec – can I get
you all to click for me……

HYPE and DJ demonstrate.

Clicking just means; I agree with you, I'm feeling this…
and if you can't click you can do the BSL for clapping…

HYPE and DJ demonstrate.

Okay now, could I get some normal applause, please…

At the back as well…

And the dress circle and balcony…

That was about a 4 out of 10, in grime raves, if an MC
smashes it – you go mental – you may attack someone you
know but in a loving way…it's kind of like…

HYPE and DJ demonstrate.

Aite, you're bored but polite…can I get you all clapping at
a 1 for a sec…

Aite, things are looking up to a 2, 3, 4 maybe it's a tennis match...5....6... 7 (I can see you at the back, come on – your Englishness is falling away) ...8...9...you're stomping, 10, brap, brap, brap, brap!

Sound effects from DJ.

Give it up for Debris Stevenson!!!!

DEBRIS: Yo Yo! What's going on? (Let's give it up for DJ Flexi and KB) You are about to hear a series of tracks, some are originals from Dizzee Rascal's album, *Boy in da Corner*, others are my interpretations of Dizzee songs.

At university I studied Byron and Shakespeare. I was taught to analyse their rhyme schemes and flow patterns as they're considered to be literary masters, but grime taught me more than the classics. Grime changed my life, more than my two first-class degrees, it gave me permission to exist and defined a groundbreaking genre, which I feel deserves to be recognised as canon, as foundation, as part of the artistic fabric of this country.

I've mimicked the rhyme scheme and flow pattern of tracks from *Boy in da Corner* starting with 'Sitting Here'. DJ Flexi play the original.

DJ starts playing 'Sitting Here' by Dizzee Rascal in background.

This is my interpretation about the life grime gifted me – working in Nottingham.

Welcome to, *Poet in the Corner.*

DJ mixes 'Sitting Here' by Dizzee Rascal into Track 1 on beat...

1. Sittin' Here: Blud Line

DEBRIS: I'm just marching back to my own yard in Notts,
    lived here ten odd years so I'm used to the kotch.
    My name's known about 'cause I teach poetry,
    to nuff of the kids; prim-ary to degree.

    I'm just trekking back – rucksack packed fulla books,
    Twenty writing jobs – I can buy a MacBook.
    When I was eleven, couldn't read a whole book,
    but now I'm a professor teaching my own book.

    When I reach my road the houses are narrow as youth;
    shirtless mandem a little uncouth;
    lounging around lightin' pound shop BBQs,
    they're sipping pon Magnums, cartons of juice.

    All the kids on my street know me, I teach poetry in their
    schools so; they call me Miss and spud me but this week
    I've been working eighteen-hour days and I just want to
    get home –

    Know when a tune reminds you – playing that 140 cross
    the street.
    Know when a tune revives you – bop a quick skank to the
    beat.
    Know when a tune rhymes with you – still rock Air Force
    1s on my feet.
    Know when a tune directs you – yeah, finally I find my
    keys.

    I see him sitting there… I see him sitting there, shiny
    Pokémon rare,
    he gives me a stare from the corner, there.
    A kid sitting there – by the bins, by the bins, by the bins.
    He's just sitting there, shiny Pokémon rare,
    he gives me a stare from the corner there,
    by the bins, by the bins, by the bins…by the bins.

So, this kid must be like thirteen years old, he's hiding in-between the two recycling bins in front of my house looks up at me (and I'm not sure where he got this from but) he abruptly asks:

KID: Yo, Miss, is you a rapper from Manchester?

DEBRIS: Sorry what…?

KID: IS–YOU–A–RAP-AH–FROM–MAN-CHES-TAH?

DEBRIS: The whole street turns from their pound shop BBQs and Argos paddling pools… How have I found a kid curled up by the bins outside my yard and I am the one getting interrogated?

Yeah, he looks straight up at me – eyes big as Charizard and Mew.
Yeah, he looks straight up at me – brandless trainers, Shoe Zone shoes.
Yeah, he looks straight up at me – I feel the whole street watching too.
Yeah, he looks straight up at me – rolls another question through.

KID: Miss?

DEBRIS: He looks at me scared – like he's got something to prove,
I look at him scared – last chance at a semblance of cool?
He looks at me scared – kids across, go to his school.
I look at him scared – they snigger and laugh at his shoes.

I want to help him, I wouldn't be standing outside my own yard if no one had ever helped me.

KID: Miss?!

DEBRIS: The best lyrics I can remember are Saw Scaled Vyper's. SS Vyper, V, was my best friend at school and this kid, curled up in chalky cat shit and rubbish – bravery

4

and oddness... It feels like he needs this, needs me, so I'm gunna go for it, like I imagine SS Vyper did the first time he was asked to spit...yeah:

Blood, you will never be the winner,
you will get eaten like a microwave dinner.
Don't cry, dry your eyes just like Mike Skinner,
Don't watch what I'm on cos you're too inna inna.
And, YEAH, nobody wants you here,
BLOOD, so why don't you go elsewhere? You –
went to your boys and they gave you AIR,
just saying what I see I'm laying it BARE!

SS VYPER stands in the circle above the stage.

SS VYPER: Are you mad?

SS VYPER turns to other audience member.

Is she mad?

DEBRIS looks on in confusion – she can't see much through the stage lights.

Yes, YOU. I'm talking to you, Deborah.

DEBRIS: Sorry...what?

SS VYPER: What do you mean 'sorry what?' – are you tryna mug me off in front of my pals?

DEBRIS: Sorry, but you're gunna have to leave...

SS VYPER: You don't remember do you? Oh my days it gets better!

So, you write a play (about me), you don't even invite me...you don't even tell me...I get here, and you're even spitting my lyrics...right now. On stage. Live.

5

DEBRIS: Hold the fuck up – can we have house lights please? PLEASE?… V?

SS VYPER: Who else did you write about and not tell or invite?

DEBRIS: It's not like that!

SS VYPER: Isn't it? Then what is it like?

DEBRIS: I just, I just, I just…

DEBRIS: I, I, I…want…wanted…but… I can explain!

SS VYPER storms out of the auditorium, pushing past audience members and slamming the door shut.

DEBRIS: Vyper. Vyper! He can't leave. Vyper please! Kirubel, please – stop him.

DEBRIS slides onto the ground – eventually into a pile in a corner.

DEBRIS hyperventilates. DJ and HYPE gather around her trying to help her to breathe.

DJ: Debris, Debris you've got to calm down. Breathe. Breathe. Can we have some help please? Nic! Nic? Stage management!

ANNOUNCEMENT: Ladies and gentlemen, we apologise for the interruption to this evening's/afternoon's performance. Please remain in your seats, the bars will remain closed at this time. We will resume as soon as possible.

DJ and stage management continue to help DEBRIS until… SS VYPER enters the auditorium stalls with HYPE.

SS VYPER: What? You didn't invite me and now you're begging me to come back.

DEBRIS: I didn't mean to… I just couldn't… I can explain. I promise I… Just let me talk to you.

HYPE: Bruv trust me I'm as confused as you are but we're never gonna get to the bottom of this if you leave. Come on just hear her out, she obviously wants to make things right.

DEBRIS: I need to start from the beginning.

SS VYPER: What could you possibly have to say that justifies this?

DEBRIS: … I can… Guys I just need your help.

HYPE: How?

DJ: I think you need to rest Debris.

DEBRIS: Please. I'm fine. Nic, Osnat I'm fine. I am so sorry everyone, we're good to continue, I just need to start again, I think, and you'll need to follow my lead…

ANNOUNCEMENT: Ladies and gentlemen, thank you for your patience. We are now ready to continue this evening's/ afternoon's performance.

DJ and HYPE decide to help DEBRIS tell her story.

2. Round We Go: Pass It On

DEBRIS: This all started before I even met you V, I was…eleven.

DJ takes us back in time seventeen years – mixing seventeen years of grime/Dizzee backwards.

HYPE: What year was that?

DEBRIS: 2001.

HYPE: Ok, so yeah, So Solid Crew drop '21 Seconds', Ruff Sqwad become a prolific grime crew.

DJ plays So Solid Crew '21 Seconds' and Ruff Sqwad.

DEBRIS: I live at home with my mum and older brother…dad was there, but not there, in a Tupperware-sized terraced house between East London and Essex. Mum vac-packed and sandwich-bagged trauma into our lunch boxes: next level claustrophobic shit.

DJ: Yeah so was Dizzee's. You know his dad died when he was two…he grew up in a single parent family on an estate in one of the most deprived areas in London: Bow. I don't think he liked it much either.

DEBRIS is eleven. 'Round we Go' by Dizzee Rascal mixes into Track 2.

DEBRIS: Osnat we're going to need some more space.

The flat flies out and the revolve moves, freaking DJ and HYPE out.

HYPE: What the hell?!

DJ: If you had this space why didn't we use it before?

DEBRIS: How many grime raves you been to with a stage this big? Stop asking questions and start helping…

DEBRIS: On 9/11 Mum spent an hour teaching me mayo to ham ratios instead of explaining what was going on… Mum wears thick glasses (plus a comedy-sized magnifying glass when reading) yet is still prettier than I can imagine being but, I'm starting to see that –

DEBRIS: Mum loves God and rules, her youth gasping for them rules/
but her kids, they question rules. Abuse calls for fight or rules.

MUM: Pass/pass/pass it on

MUM/DEBRIS: Pass/pass/pass it on

ALL: Pass/pass/pass it on

MUM: Pass your trauma till it's gone.

DEBRIS: Pass/pass/pass it on. Pass/pass/pass it on
pass/pass/pass it on. Pass your trauma till it's gone.

First, she was homeless –
Italy to Egypt/Egypt to East End/
was alone eating/packed lunch weeping/
as caretaker's sweeping
– in the dinner hall.

Mum's poor English – school's hard to fin-ish,
she was the oldest – cared for her siblings,
airtight feelings – packing and sealing
– can't breathe through it all.

Mum is a daughter, of a Jew's daughter, of a war's daughter,
(hereditary trauma?) She has one daughter – never hit me,
she's a pacifist – whose one son who grew,
questioned her food/then got a bit rude
started diggin' up clues/unpackin' her rules,
– she didn't know what to do.

She's good with kids/in a look forbids/
my bro's power trips/inside we hid –
inna thoughts lose grip/she wants it her way
– so, she can rule.

Dad lets her rule,
says nuffin at all,
just follows her rules.

TONY: Emotional jam/this isn't our jam?

DEBRIS: Mum packed us tall/
Dad's at work for it all/
we're feeling full/
I feel too full?

MUM: Mum loves God and rules, her youth gasping for dem rules/
but her kids –

DEBRIS/TONY: We question rules.

MUM: Abuse calls for fight or rules.
Pass/pass/pass it on. Pass/pass/pass it on
pass/pass/pass it on. Pass this trauma till it's gone.

DEBRIS/TONY: Pass/pass/pass it on? Pass pass/pass it on?
Pass/pass/pass it on? Pass your trauma till it's… ?

3. Jus' a Rascal (But He Locks His Door)

DEBRIS: Dear Heavenly Father, I thank you for this day, the pack
lunch Mum so kindly made, and all my many blessings…but
please can you help me with the book Tony gave me, I want
to know if Matilda beats Miss Trunchbull but all the letters
keep…moving. I promise I will remember this lesson and
apply it to my daily life, in the name of Jesus Christ, Amen.

… Telling stories, speaking, that's how I understand
everything, but…reading? I don't even know where to begin.

TONY: What do you mean, it's easy.

DEBRIS: Not really… If I'm speaking I'm sprinting, then as
soon as I look at a book – I hit water, I'm drowning.

TONY: You know, if you think you're stupid, you inevitably will
be.

DEBRIS: At eleven, my older brother is my key non-Mormon
educational resource. He tells me things like –

TONY: Winston Churchill, a former Prime Minister once said
– 'In order to be a great man, one must first become a great
rascal.'

DEBRIS: But Tony is biased because…

> Bruva's a rascal – jus' a rascal – Tony's a rascal – elder rascal,
> Tony's a rascal, I'm his disciple, so I think I too gotta be a
> rascal.

> Bruva Tony's 5 foot 6 – he never forgives,
> Mumzie 'cause she fuelled him vegetarian – till he was six.

> And Tony he was suspended for hacking into Barclays bank,
> and Tony he was arrested – rewiring a street-lamp.

> And Tony, yes, he was detained – for selling BB guns,
> and Tony he was making P – from marijuana funds.

> Tony's a genius – so I don't go his school,
> Mumzie said –

MUM: No 11+, 'cause you're not clever enough.

DEBRIS: I'm not clever enough? I'm not clever enough?

> Mumzie said –

MUM: No 11+, 'cause you're not clever enough.

DEBRIS: I looked at Dad to defend me, desperate to go to
a school where I knew someone… I don't know what I
expected but, he just took off his Royal Mail jacket and went
upstairs to rest before his evening shift in the sorting office.

> Tony's a genius – twist PlayStation into PCs – serious,
> serious – ballsy, bolts his door – ignores Mumzie – jacks
> off chores.

> Going to grammar school, dashing his door, shouting at
> Mumzie, what for?
> Giving me advice I'm too dumb for – *bruv, bruv,* (but he
> locks his door).

It's okay for Tony, he's some mad Matilda – swimming through every book in the house by the time he's eight. But he's just ripped my armbands off and dashed me in his swimming pool and expecting me to swim when –

I'm not a rascal – yet a rascal, I'm not a rascal, younger rascal. I'm not a rascal – I'm his disciple.

But he's at grammar school –
so, what do I do? What do I do?

When I can't keep up with Tony to grammar, I turn to Seven Kings, the best secondary school in the borough – right next to my house. Then, they build a massive council estate…

Estate at back of the stage revealed.

…on the other side of the Iron Bridge in-between my house and Seven Kings. So, Seven Kings cut their catchment area to 2min on one side so no one on the estate and beyond can go there.

As a result, I'm sent to the worst school in the neighbouring borough – a forty-five minute commute and only one other girl I know from my primary school, called Garminder…

4. All The Best Storytellers Are Liars

DEBRIS: It's the 1st of April, 2002, my twelfth birthday.

HYPE: Erm… More Fire Crew drop 'Oi!' and Heartless Crew drop 'Heartless Theme'. Wiley's first 'Eskimo' dance takes place in Area nightclub. Brappp! I'm good at this!

'Oi!' by More Fire Crew plays mixed with 'Eskimo' by Wiley then 'Heartless Theme'.

DEBRIS: I'm starting to question the lines between 'truth', story, religion and my mum… Reality stops seeming reliable.

DJ: Uncanny! Dizzee also started to question the people around him what was once gospel. He got pulled off a moped and stabbed four times in the chest in Napa (narrowly missing his vital organs) and he felt like his community at the time didn't have his back which was the start of his ongoing beef with (Wiley).

HYPE pushes BEEEEEEEP SFX.

I'm good at it too!

DEBRIS: Mum dictates me to sleep; Bible, Carroll, Mormon, Dahl. It's either Audiobooks or her own stories, like how she got arrested for riding a moped with a colander on her head instead of a helmet. Mum's creative with reality; she records educational TV on VHS then replays it on evenings and weekends (for years we thought that's just what TV was?)

It's my twelfth Birthday (or is it?)
I wake up worried (or do I?)
Mum puts a blur on reality like
reciting all her best stories at night.

TONY: She's having an 'episode'… I've read about this stuff… You know something is wrong with Mum because when she gets happy, I get scared.

DEBRIS: What's an episode?

TONY: Look, D –

All the best storytellers are liars, liars/best storytellers are liars, liars,
best storytellers are liars, liars, liars, liars, liars.

All the best storytellers are liars, liars/best storytellers are liars, liars.

The best storytellers are liars, lions, liars, tigers and bears.

DEBRIS: So, I go to a school where I don't know jack –
lonely as an empty sandwich bag,
Mum gives me a Mormon badge –
Caucasian Jesus, slyly stacked.

MUM: Happy Birthday my sunbean bag –

DEBRIS: And I head off to school with my big backpack.

In my first month at school, I didn't say anything to anyone, I just focus on getting through the kettled hallways then finding Garminder to sit next to at the back (I didn't say anything to her either – it was just nice for at least one thing to feel familiar). That was, until Tiana Bustos-Beltrain says –

TIANA: Hi –

DEBRIS: And hugs me out of nowhere.

TIANA: I've seen you alone – that's not right! You want to come chill with me? I went to the primary school round the corner so I know everyone (and my big brother is in MOD in Year 11 so they all listen to me too)!

DEBRIS: MOD?

TIANA: Oh, you are fresh! The Ministry of Darkness! It's the biggest crew in the school.

DEBRIS: Tiana was full of information…she made me feel welcome; taught me how to roll up my school skirt, do my fat/short tie and slick my hair down with a soft brush and Pink. She even came to my house and spoke to Mum in Colombian Spanish! I finally have a place… I can't wait to see what she got me for my birthday, I'd bet you money it's not Jesus-themed!

14

I usually meet Tiana before form class outside the sports hall where she hands out stolen Freddo bars from the Happy Shopper with the pervert at the counter… Shoot, I'm late –

DEBRIS runs down the hallway, she sees TIANA who barges into her, tipping her big backpack over her like a tortoise.

TIANA: Deborah, Deborah this ain't a game,
Tiana I ain't your friend – these lot feel the same.
That girl Deborah touched Amir's dick,
that girl Deborah she's a racist.

Wait, what colour are you?

DEBRIS: I say white and they say it's not true,
so, I say Italian – they look confused.
Tiana says racist – claims not proved.

TIANA: Oi, what colour are you?
What are Mormons/what are you?
Why do you talk like that/do you
have money/nah, wait, look at her shoes.

DEBRIS: I have no idea what's going on, when I get to form class Amna (Tiana's best friend) is already sitting next to Garminder so I have to sit next to Rajpal who ignores me when I ask to borrow her rubber. It feels like I've swallowed a fist full of chip shop chips, I hold my breath to stop the tears falling out my face. What did I do? I don't understand?

TIANA: Deb thinks she's black – got an Afro-pick,
slicks her hair with grease – Pink.
I went to her house – psychopathic.
Mum pretends to speak Spanish.

DEBRIS: Form's done/I spring out fast as a hunted stag/I feel Tiana on by back/I hold my breath (like a kid in a wardrobe in *Goosebumps*). I just want to get to science class/if I can just get to science class I can get fifty-five minutes to work out what to do/I see the edge of the science block/get my breathe out like a long piss but then it comes like a door's creek...

Tiana starts calling my name from the other side of the field, over and over and over....

TIANA: Oi... Deborah? Deborah?... DEBORAH?

DEBRIS: And of all people, it's Garminder, standing next to Tiana that says –

GARMINDER: DEBORAH! I ain't your friend anymore now either.

DEBRIS: So, I run to disabled toilet/pound my fists into the walls/ haul this slicked hair from my scalp/rip dis shit tiny tie out I stamp and kick and thrash about and all the ceiling toilet roll fucking falls down
and it's wet and mouldy and stinks of brown –

ARRRRRRGGGGGGGGGHHHHHHHHHHHH –

TIANA bangs on toilet door.

TIANA: Coward! See, she wouldn't be hiding if she wasn't a liar! DEBORAH – we've had enough of your stories, you have no friends here, stay out of everyone's way, I don't care if you have to stay in here all day. I don't want to ever have to hear your voice or see your face, okay?

DEBRIS: I wait in the toilet, covered in brown, damp tissue till the last school bell rings. I walk home the back way. When I get home... I've forgotten my keys... I lay on the recycling bins outside the house and cry till Mum gets home.

MUM: Ciao! Happy birthday baba! Look what I made you!

MUM doesn't notice that DEBRIS has been crying and just hands her a fluffy, cream, ill-fitting jumper with an embroidered depiction of an unusually sexy and ginger Jesus.

DEBRIS: Wow, right…thanks, Mum.

So, she gives me this mad jumper and all I can think to
say is –

Mum, I think I'm getting bullied.

She smiles, like a creepy Disney/politician hybrid smile AKA
The Mormon Classic and quotes a Shakespearean sonnet she
memorised on a free course at Redbridge Library –

MUM: 'Shall you pace forth; your praise shall still find room/
even in the eyes of all posterity/That wear this world out
to the ending doom.' It's about supreme love, if we had
this kind of love, we'd not have war – the kind of love
Christ had really.

DEBRIS: Wrap it up, put it in your lunch box and pass it
on, init. Mum's good at telling stories, not so good at
assimilating the truth.

DEBRIS/TONY: All the best storytellers are liars, liars/best
storytellers are liars, liars,
The best storytellers are liars, lions, liars, tigers and bears.
The best storytellers are liars, liars/best storyteller's prophesies.
The best storytellers are liars, liars, pious, mothers and heirs.

5. Tag Team Ladder Match

DEBRIS: 2003. I'm thirteen, I've been hiding in the library
from Tiana for a good year.

HYPE: Dizzee and Crazy Titch clash on Deja Vu FM, it's
caught on the infamous 'Conflict DVD'. Channel U
is launched.This is one of the first times the public are
actually able to see the faces of the MCs they've been
listening to.

Boy in da Corner is released and goes on to win a Mercury Prize, one of two grime albums ever to do so. Dun Kno!

Audio clip of Crazy T and Dizzee Rascal clashing on the Deja rooftop.

DEBRIS: This is the year that I met you Vyper, I was living in the library on my ones and watching you was the closest thing to an education I could find.

DJ: You know Dizzee was excluded from every class at school except music? His teacher Tim Smith, got him making his own productions on a classroom computer and writing bars, on the *Boy in da Corner* album sleeve, it says, 'Special thanx to Mr. Smith, da best music teacher Langdon Park ever let go (you fools). I'll never forget da way you kept the faith in me, even when things looked grim.'

DJ sound effect: DING, DING, Round 1 –

Lonely – Tesco – Value – bourbons inna library, I'm stuttering primary.
I am my own – audiobook, but I'm all chewed up like an exercise book.
Mum-packed-lunches – pre-cooked – the playground I overlook.
Are all omnipotent narrators shook? I mutter to myself with no notebook.

DJ sound effect: DING, DING, Round 2 –

But – den – wrestling finds me, Smack Down book from a Year 13.
WWE – status, teams, enemies – favourites – Matt and Jeff Hardy,
climbing buildings, mounting dreams, ladders stacked high as a bright sun beam.

DJ sound effect: DING, DING Round 3 –

– Fellow library loner sees this fetish,
pokes my shoulder – turn, tentative.

HYPE pokes DEBRIS on the shoulder and begins sitting down to be SS VYPER.

SS VYPER: Nah, nah, nah… Tonight Matthew I'm going to be… ME. You lot tried to do this play without me and NOW you wanna tell me how I lived MY life!

Smoke machine and wheel up of track. HYPE tags in SS VYPER. DJ gives SS VYPER cheap walkman and headphones with a stack of cassette tapes to pass on to DEBRIS.

DEBRIS: I think you said…

SS VYPER: You're not the only one that was there you know!

If you like that – then you'll like this – it's like wrestling but wiv ly-rics.

DEBRIS: What's this?

SS VYPER: It's music?

DEBRIS: Is it… Garage?

DJ plays garage snippet, cut off by SS VYPER.

SS VYPER: No, it hasn't really got a name…

DEBRIS: Where did you get it?

SS VYPER: I recorded it off Rinse.

DEBRIS: Who's that?

DJ plays pirate radio montage from 2003.

SS VYPER: IT is a pirate radio station set up by DJ Slimzee, he scaled rooftops higher dan anyfin Matt or Jeff Hardy ever jumped off: climbed whole tower blocks and shimmied up pipes at night to reach us, to play this to us, to represent us, that's what pirate radio was invented for ya know.

DJ sound effect: Wrestling crowd go wild.

A little montage of DEBRIS listening to Dizzee Rascal on tapes.

DEBRIS: Radio is even better than wrestling…because some of the MCs go to my school. Radio is definitely better than church because –

SS VYPER: MCs write bars in either 8's, 16's, 32's, or 64's – basically if you can understand that there's four beats in a bar, it's easy. The shorter the bar is the more catchy it has to be, so if you're writing an 8 bar, then keep it simple – these are the singalongs that make you big (basically choruses init). If you got stuff to get off your chest then obviously the bars gunna be longer – like a 32 or a 64. Look I'll show you.

WATCH – I'm gunna break your face
Then hang you with your own shoelace
Even your own boys call you waste I'm
Too on point observing the place ANNNNND
Nah, you don't wanna come against me I'm a
Lyrical G – you're a waste MC
Won't make sense for us to clash 'cause you will
Get eaten like bangers and mash.

DJ sound effect: DING, DING, Round 4 –

DEBRIS: SS Vyper – shit – I've heard rumours about his wit – taught himself four languages – walked in radio, just a kid,

Saw a door ajar and he wandered in – they gave him the mic thought they'd get rid,
but he blew up the set at just twelve years – he's the pirate radio terrorist.

I stop seeing Ezekiel AKA SS Vyper in the library reading encyclopaedias soon after his pirate radio debut circulates the school. So, I have to up my pace to try catch him on our joint commute – I loudly flick through my Pokédex at the bus stop, 'cause I see his cards bulging from his front pocket.

SS VYPER: Strong collection.

DEBRIS: Thanks, hand-me-down from my brother.

SS VYPER: I'm the oldest.

DEBRIS: Youngest.

SS VYPER: I'm a Saw Scaled Vyper, SS Vyper, V – smallest snake responsible for the most fatalities init.

DEBRIS: I'm...just, Deborah.

SS VYPER: Deborah...? Just, Deborah. Hmmmm... Deb... Deb...ree? Deb-ree... Debris, yeah, sick. Das what I'll call ya. Everyone needs an MC name... You look low-key capable of destruction – Debris, that cool?

DEBRIS: Very.

DEBRIS and SS VYPER start coincidentally walking to and from school together on a regular, but they part ways once they enter the school gates.

SS Vyper makes donations –
his pirate cassettes off all stations,
talk other shit like Pokémon –
only en route to school and home.

He's got friends and I'm alone.
He's got friends and I'm alone.
He's got friends and I'm alone.
He's not gunna chill wiv a library gnome.

SS VYPER: You seen the Charizard shiny Jasdeep paid a bill for?

DEBRIS: I don't know what a bill is but as he talks to me I'm completed, where once I was drowning – I now have a life jacket.

I pull my Pokémon wodge, like a gangsta with a roll of fifties elastic banded together and I slip it straight in his top pocket.

SS VYPER: Debris – whatchu doin? Woah, you sure?

DEBRIS: Am I sure? 'Am I just some whore banging on ya door, what for?'

SS VYPER: 'Pregnant what you talking 'bout be sure?'

ALL: 'FIFTEEN SHE'S UNDERAGE THAT'S RAW! AND AGAINST LAW FIVE YEARS OR MORE!'

SS VYPER: Actually, got sumfin for you too –

DJ sound effect: DING, DING, Round 5 –

SS VYPER passes DEBRIS a copy of 'Boy in da Corner', the seam fixed with gaffer tape.

DEBRIS: How did you even get this?

SS VYPER: Inherited from my cuz init.

DEBRIS: I can't.

SS VYPER: You have to, I want to see how many words you been getting wrong now we don't have any static to fight through.

DEBRIS: Dizzee Rascal's always been my favourite – Dizzee gets that I'm bullied, that I'm lonely and he tells stories like my Dahl audiobooks, even Mum's audio Bible. Dizzee's as honest and raw as wrestling and radio but I've only ever heard Dizzee 2D, cassettes recorded and rewound till faulty. This CD case has a broken spine, hinged together with tape…makes sense – bit a gaffer, because corners are where broken things gather.

6. Fix Up, Look Sharp Part 1. Personalised Encyclopaedia

SS VYPER: Oh come on, you ain't in no corner – you got ham and cheese in your home-made wholemeal sandwiches! If you think your life is bad –

DEBRIS: Try being a Mormon!

SS VYPER: Try living on the estate!

DEBRIS: Try having parents that wear magic underwear over their underwear: I don't know what sex is?

SS VYPER: Try having a Year 7 on a push bike punch you in the face and rip your chaps from your neck at the bus stop –

DEBRIS: I wish my mum would punch me in the face –

SS VYPER: I'm saving up for a 'ped.

DEBRIS: Why don't you just tell your cuz?

SS VYPER: I don't actually wanna fight…

DEBRIS: I can fight you if you want? You be Jeff, I'll be Matt – winner has the most fucked up life!

Look at least you're good at stuff, got a cousin looking out for you…

SS VYPER: I guess…

DEBRIS: …and you got bars… Everything I want! So, stop moaning!

SS VYPER: What I want is to write about history or politics –
stuff that changes or documents history… I spent all that
time reading whatever I could get my hands on in the
library and it was all interesting, but nothing ever spoke
to me. Like, who's writing the history for my family, the
estate, schools like this?

DEBRIS: I've heard your lyrics – that's what you're doing!

SS VYPER: I'm not sure people like me write history.

DEBRIS: What do you mean?

DJ plays crickets – awkward silence.

SS VYPER: Oi, what's this then? Looks like you DO have bars!

*SS VYPER pulls DEBRIS' lyric book out of her pocket and flicks
through it.*

These are good man! Spit me something…

DEBRIS: Allow me mannnnn!

SS VYPER: Try me –

*DJ and HYPE start clapping and stomping 'Fix Up, Look Sharp'
rhythm for DEBRIS to spit to then the DJ slowly comes in.*

DEBRIS: I'd heard the bullies from the field to the Dixy –
I heard them shouting, shouting till Dizzee.
Being a grime MC feels like a fantasy,
fuck'a preconceptions I'ma be a solo lesson.

'Cause I was peeling from the ceiling –
lobbed like wet tissue but I felt myself setting.
Run towards the beef, like fishes to a reef?
Baby hair sticking 'n' Nike trackies dropping.

SS VYPER: Vyper's never been the roughest;
Rasket told me to fix up and look sharp it made me tougher;

24

When it comes to words I say a line and cause a ruckus now I'm
Known across the borough by uncles cousins and
Mothers;

Still ain't makin sense then yo can go and ask your brother;
bet he don't believe you bet he laughs at you or stutters;
If it wasn't for Rasket I wouldn't be causing rackets feet still
On the ground I gotta have my siblings home by supper;

DEBRIS: I'd sit on the street watch like a piranha,
  when the spitter's spat, I'd sweat inside like shawarma.
  I was not ready for his flow –
  guts, order heart sober, hear Captain Rascal!

  Not a peng gyal, smart gyal but a spitta spitta –
  with a disc cut into my blazer,
  looped lyrics – clash with Asha,
  hear his voice, I'm not an outsider.

SS VYPER: Far from your normal kid, I was
  In my yard when all the kids were playing on the swings
  Sitting in cousins whip; listening to Rinse when I heard
  Dizzee I was going sick behind the tints;

  Not I one to repeat I know he
  Said a lot of things; but from I
  Heard *Boy in da Corner* I been different ever since;
  sittin' 'ere tryna hold my mouth was never it, so I'm just
  using all the words, so I can give you lot a glimpse.

7. Respect My Struggle

SS VYPER: Hold up. Stop. Stooppp!! That was really sweet,
  but it's not true. I love how you skipped over my struggle
  and emphasised yours. My life wasn't that easy and

carefree.
It wasn't all singalongs and laughter.

You're gunna re
Spect my struggle…respect my
Struggle; you and I come from two
Different worlds; I ain't in your bubble
Might both come from the same
Place but we got two different hustles;
Your pain ain't nothing like my
Pain is that's two different troubles

You're gunna re
Spect my struggle…respect my
Struggle; you and I come from two
Different worlds; I ain't in your bubble
Might both come from the same
Place but we got two different hustles;
Your pain ain't nothing like my
Pain is that's two different troubles

Upset cos you don't wanna go home;
Upset cos you go school on ya own;
Couldn't go school with your badbreed bro?
What about the poor kids? Sorry?
Oh?

Ungrateful what the hell do you know?
You ain't ever sold no drugs in the cold.
You ain't ever been rushed on ya way home; you got a
way out none of this I

Chose; upset cos your mum don't like
Fighting; leave home and all I see is
Violence; uphill struggle every day I'm
Climbing; white girls ain't gotta worry 'bout

Trident;

Black boys don't get peace or silence;
Just get threatens with the piece or
Silenced; bet you a grand you don't know what
Crime is, you are not like this and I know you

Said you wanna be an MC but being an M
C don't make you the same;
I'm a black boy who ain't welcome in a lotta
Places nothing ain't changed;
So many places I don't feel safe but, you
Wanna invade MY space?
I'm V when I'm 'ere; V when I go home for
you this is just an escape so 'low all the

Talk; you're too ambiguous you
Thought that we believe you're living this but
No, I see through smoke and mirrors so just
Slow; our lives are two different
Shows; same place but we got different
Goals; end of the day you're chilling at home;
End of the day I'm still tryna get doe…

DEBRIS: So, that's what it is yeah?
    Your misery trumps mine?
    Your struggle is worse every time?
    Dagenham statistics, shine –

    Bottom of the ladder Caribbean and White
    Cockney and Patois – combine.
    Is grime's journey some straight line?
    Neither – is yours or mine.

    I am beside you in dis fight.
    Black British music I recognise;

Dancehall, Dub and Sound system
are the grandchildren: Windrush generation…
Patois' paving – East London,
Cockney's saying *wagwan son*
Don't even know where dat saying came from.
White working class, can't be a cousin? But –

SS VYPER: So you're gonna respect my –

DEBRIS: Struggle…respect my
Struggle; you and I come from two
Different worlds; I ain't in your bubble
Might both come from the same
Place but we got two different hustles;
Your pain ain't nothing like my
Pain is this is two different troubles.

Scratchy, Logan, Devlin –
Syer B, Skittlez or Flava D
Intersection: class 'n' immigration.
A black boy I don't claim to be.

Look – grime it shaped me.
Look – grime it cured me.
Look – grime's something different to me.
Ain't the godfather or claiming to be –

YES – you took me to radio,
YES – that showed me where to go,
YES – grime has inspired me,
like the best art does successfully.

YES – I've been through shit.
YES – without grime I couldn't survive it.
YES – been ignorant to your side of it.
BUT – didn't I deserve to escape this? –

8. Fix Up, Look Sharp Part 2. Doom

MUM's kitchen.

DEBRIS: We sit obediently in the kitchen (aka the sexy
gentrified Jesus gift shop) waiting for breakfast. This is the
last remaining place my family all sit together in the house…

See, Mum is Boss Level 1:

MUM: Dear Heavenly Father, and his son
Thank you for this food, some have none.

DEBRIS: Brother's eyes open, arms undone –
Mum's in work clothes…
her apron holds her together –

MUM: We thank you for who put this together
and those who receive it, those we treasure.

DEBRIS: Dad, *Amen*, Mum, *Amen*, Me, *Amen* and then
and then, and then, and then –

my brother starts laughing/laughing/laughing –

TONY: How can you chat shit wivout creasing?

DEBRIS: First swear word at the table – ceasing.
I look up at Mum – nothing, nothing.
Expression from her face – draining,
Game console – staring.

– I see her walking so slow it's a hover,
floats to the fridge, opens the door slower,
looking inside pupils wide as a sea
goes for the milk – semi-skimmed kidnapper.
– I see her whole body tensing,
feet to floor Tony is still laughing.
Navigating round, the kitchen is her playground

29

moving so tight he looks up, she's against him.
– Mum grabs face like a tune
his neck strains back I'm not sure what to do,
milk carton in/she puts throttle in
like a kiss feed but he is choking.
– He starts gulp-ing
tries to lean back but he is drowning.
He's gunna die, yeah, my brother's gunna die.
Turning water white, you could call it waterboarding.
Meanwhile, Dadzie's munching on his breakfast
too distracted wiv getting food on his bestest.
– But my brother is alone.
My hero trying, milk streaming from his nose.
– If my bruva can't KO this level,
how can I eva get outta this level?
Might as well be Dad hiding in cereal.
I catch my bruva's eyes let him know dis is real.
Look at me, bruv, we're in dis together,
– If you can drink dat milk, we'll get out together.
Right now, I'm finkin Matilda,
that kid Brucie wiv the cake and the pressure.
And my eyes say it –
bruva you can do it,
If you just chug it.
Like that fat kid,
you got all of the strength,
if you just chug it.

And the milk – he chugs it, chugs it
the milk – he chugs it, chugs it
the milk – he chugs it, chugs it
chugs it, chugs it, chugs it,
chugs it, chugs it, chugs it.

– Till it's just a bubble – a final gargle,
kid on a chewed-up straw in trouble,
defiant as a carton of milk to Thatcher
looking at me – thank ya.

I'm not saying a word past Mum but he gets it,
Tony sitting taller than gentrified Jesus,
cheeky as a cheat code, Jesus.
Dad finally stops eating his breakfast.

Mum crosses her arms –
closes her eyes, I uncross mine
as they bless the food,
Tony he dines:

grabs his toast that's been baptized
in semi-skimmed milk – right!
Boss Level 1 KO'd – rise.
Dad, *Amen.* Mum, *Amen.* Me,
                          – Amen?
And then, and then, and then...

9. To Be Crazy

DEBRIS: Mum says, there will always be someone bigger and
    stronger
        – the only way to win, is to be crazy... She'll do anything.
    I scream into my pillow till the blood vessels in my corners
    crack: sputter my skin. I thought she was going to kill him.

    I laid awake most of the night listening to Tony next door
    packing,
    he doesn't say goodbye, doesn't want a rematch.
    I'm alone with a woman that could literally turn to anything.

31

My room, so small I can hear my breath catch

on the walls. There are new rules pitched as sin –
doors aren't even closed to sleep.
The only thing keeping my head above semi-skimmed
is the Walkman Tony leaves behind. Only person I got at
home now, is Dizzee –

a bigger, stronger and crazier sound than I can conceive,
than Mum can conceive – he's training me
in batshit bass-ridden bravery
as my sputtered skin fades slowly.

10. Stop Dat: Ask Why

DEBRIS: 2004. I'm fourteen years old.

HYPE: Lethal Bizzle Releases 'Pow', achieving a top 20 hit.
People go so crazy for the tune that club promoters go to
lengths to ban it in their venues because of the crowd's
reaction.

DJ: Lord of the Mics and Risky Roadz DVDs are released –
changing the way the music was being consumed forever.

*DJ mixes 'Pow' by Lethal Bizzle and audio clips from Lord of the
Mics and Risky Roads.*

DEBRIS: *Boy in da Corner*, wasn't just an album, it was a
philosophy – it was permission to be different, to be
outspoken, to tell a story…my story. But all of that was a
fantasy without you – you taught me how to 'Stand Up
Tall' in real time. Do you remember…?

'Stop Dat' by Dizzee Rascal plays:

SS VYPER: So, I'm called into Ms. Greenwood's office.

DEBRIS: Your head of year?

SS VYPER: Yeah.

DEBRIS: What's she saying?

SS VYPER: Some tantrum about me bussing a lift with you and your mum to school!

DEBRIS: Rah, that was quick – she cussing you for missing registration? Bruh, nothing even happens in that fifteen minutes anyway –

SS VYPER: Nothing might happen for YOU in that fifteen mins…
They didn't wanna care,
left man sitting in a class somewhere.
Too many assholes, not enough chairs
and more time I just wanna be elsewhere.
And I don't think the same so I come across weird.
Talk to the teachers but they don't care.
No, we ain't equal no it ain't fair cos a
textbook don't do shit around 'ere.

So missing registration, means missing; rush hour, trekking to d bus stop, getting the bus, kotching in traffic – so it ain't just fifteen mins, D – that lift means, after I get up at six a.m. and do my paper round, I can have a nap before I drop my brother and sister to school, or make Mum's lunch, or write a tune, or catch up on coursework. That's prime real estate time in my yard you know!

DEBRIS: What Ms. Greenwood say?

SS VYPER: She expects betta.

Stop dat start dat get that (what).
Vibes in the air man feels that (what).
Text in the flesh dat's freedom (what).

Who said that I can't do that? (what).
Words full of truth no paper (what).
Trapped in print like a victim (what).
Till I broke out of the system (what).
Education made me a misfit (what).

So, Ms. Greenwood says – in the 'real world', I need to
know when to be on time.

DEBRIS: HA! What they teaching us about the real world
in here? I got locked in maths for four hours last week
because someone let off two cans of CS gas in the hallway!

SS VYPER: I say to her, yeah – I got a paper round in the
mornings, work lunchtimes in Gary's burger van, plus I
take my bruva and sister to school and I still get A's… I
look 'er in the eye and say, 'It's a shame dis real world ain't
grading us on practical efficiency of time management over
dis bullshit box ticking theory'.

Charlie Sloth 'smashed it' sound from DJ decks.

DEBRIS: Shittttt – You duck out?

SS VYPER: I was tempted…but I thought, calm, in her utter
shock it felt like there was an opportunity, so I say to her,
all calm and nice and that – 'Look, Miss, I like you ya
know. But, as one of the only kids getting A's in dis school,
I find it's in all of our interests that I'm as well rested as
possible. Maybe you could talk to my form tutor about
registration, I'm happy to pop in at the beginning of first
period and tell her I'm in.'

DEBRIS: Shitttttt.

SS VYPER: Den I walked out before her jaw fully dislocated.

More celebratory sound effects from the decks.

Getting punished for making the best out of a bad
situation – there must be something better than this for us?

DEBRIS: I think if there is, we might have to work it out for
ourselves though.

SS VYPER: Stop dat start dat get that (what).
Vibes in the air man feels that (what).
Text in the flesh dat's freedom (what).
Who said that I can't do that? (what).
Words full of truth no paper (what).
Trapped in print like a victim (what).
Till I broke out of the system (what).
Education made me a misfit (what).

11. Polygamy

DEBRIS: The Mormon Church is getting really shit press –
everyone at school asks –

DJ: Yo, has your dad got more than one wife?

DEBRIS and MUM at home, in the kitchen.

DEBRIS: Rumours. What do I say? Mum?
Humming hymns to herself in the kitchen,
peeling parsnips in the evening sun.
But Mum, if no one's practicing polygamy, where are the
rumours coming from?

Okay…hmmm, okay…right. Wait, sorry, what…aye?
WE USED TO BE POLYGAMOUS?
Couldn't God of all people provide another way to repopulate
the faith without breaking the law of chastity?
Did Joseph Smith pray to Heavenly Father and Heavenly
Father

said, Thou shalt be able to sleep with whoever thy wants?!
What the actual ffffff – you teach me to defend your saviour
but you have never told me what I'm defending? … What,
no response?

Mum peels white flesh through tears: oven prep. This is
ridiculous.
Gas consumes our corridor-sized kitchen…has this
conversation ended? Serious –
You're not even gonna hug me in the name of God, nah?
Mum? Ha –
I wish we did still practice polygamy…so I'd have someone
to turn to right now, rah.

Hypocrites, fucking hypocrites. Do you know how many
times my mum's sent me to school with a speech to
defend HER CHURCH but without explaining any of
this!? She's been preaching how and when it's convenient.
I've been defending a bunch of ball – laughed at for
nothing but lies. AND Mum would sooner PEEL A
ROOT VEGETABLE than talk to me honestly about it.
Arrrrrgggggghhhhhhhhhhhhhhhh.

DEBRIS puts her headphones on and screams into her pillow.

Cut back to bunking in the school field.

12. Jezebel: Baptism By Immersion

DEBRIS: 2005, I'm fifteen.

HYPE: 'P's and Q's' by Kano is released.

DJ plays 'P's & Q's' by Kano.

Founder of the pirate radio station, Rinse FM, DJ Slimzee is given an ASBO, banning him from every rooftop in Tower Hamlets.

Form 696 is given to venues by the Met police, it asks for details such as the ethnic groups of the audiences and the performer's name, address and date of birth as a means of 'risk assessment' – shutting down many grime events.

DEBRIS: The way religion was programmed into my body – it's like I was locked into it – I bathed with my clothes on and undressed in the wardrobe for years. I was scared of even my own body let alone someone else's! And that discomfort in my own body meant I always felt like an outsider, like I was one of the boys or one of the girls or an MC or a library geek or just that kid in the corner with a notebook. It took me some time to get out of the box I was put in.

DJ: I bet Dizzee felt like that too, going from Bow to the king of underground going commercial; he supported Justin Timberlake and the Red Hot Chili Peppers. Some people say he sold out, but I think he's just always done what he wanted to do, always writing the realness of what he sees regardless/ he never let anyone put him in a box.

DEBRIS is lying on the school field with SS VYPER and the mandem listening to the 'Jezebel' chorus by Dizzee Rascal.

DEBRIS: It's the first time I've ever bunked off class and my boys are explaining what a 'jezebel' is –

SS VYPER: Skets, hoes, jezebels, jezes; girls dat 'ave been 'twanged' –

JONATHAN: Sweet talked into handing things over.

SS VYPER: Twanging is the act of seeming interested but onna sly –

JONATHAN: Out of d public eye –

SS VYPER: Making jeze think you like her.

JONATHAN: Den using that to get 'tings' from her –

SS VYPER: Like head or group sex or treating her like shit in
school but banging her in every private opportunity. Soon
come, the twanger will tell everyone at school what jeze
did, and no one will touch jeze –

JONATHAN: In a meaningful way.

SS VYPER: Again.

JONATHAN: Like, if you give head or if you're too easy to
break into –

SS VYPER: Your wifey career is over –

JONATHAN: We all know that, so these girls…

SS VYPER: Jezes –

JONATHAN: Their behaviour is ridiculous to me…how can
they not tell a twanger is chattin' shit?

DEBRIS: A jeze sits next to me, Jonathan passes her a zoot, all
the mandem are bunning and bussing jokes, she must fink
we are her friends 'cause she's flowing into me, so close
I can see these three freckles in a triangle on her right
earlobe…she smells like Lynx, weed and bacon rolls, her
skin is like the sand in a country I can't afford to go to.

Everyone is high except me, Jeze speaks into my face so
close she's blurry, her lips ripple the fine hairs on my face,
I can hear her breathin' deep and melodic as the lake in
Barking Park. We've stopped talking, Jeze looks into me,
loops her whole hand around my pinky and pulls me in
closer, each breath a wave lapping against my skin…my
eyes submerge, warm blue laps at my lips –

Boys burst out laughing, Jeze hits them till they shut up.

– Jeze holds her breath, we both open, inhale sharp, she pulls
away, starts laughing too. Jeze looks at me and for a moment
– I think she might understand something I don't quite get
yet but before she can speak Jonathan gets up, takes her hand
and they dissolve into a mesh of metal and tarmac behind
the basketball courts.

I was told sex was evil and it dragged my body under:
a locked car into water – sealed in by pressure.
        Then girls like Jeze let men come down –
helmets, crowbars, ripped her doors down.
She makes it look easy – people swim in freely.

    But I'll never be dat free (I'd be a bulletproof vest at
a house party)
    I can feel pleasure encroaching on me;
orgasms a threat of burglary, bolt cutters breaking into
me, church
put a deadlock into me, bathed in my clothes
till thirteen (shame).

ALL: Shame –

DEBRIS: Even love feels like a break in.

ALL: Shame –

DEBRIS: Jeze on'a courts covered in him.

ALL: Shame –

DEBRIS: She took me by the face kissed me in public till I felt
    safe –

ALL: shame.

DEBRIS: Jeze stepped back, everyone laughing – they went
    mad, next thing I know she's going on bad, took my boy
    Jonathan straight round the back.

DEBRIS: Jeze, what did he do?

SS VYPER: You didn't let him…

JONATHAN: What?

DEBRIS: What?

SS VYPER: Sket ting,

JONATHAN: (Man already said she's nothing).

DEBRIS: Seen her crying in the ladies.

SS VYPER: Lady's all she wants to be.

JONATHAN: She clings.

DEBRIS: (Man already said she's nothing).

SS VYPER: Seen her crying in the ladies.

JONATHAN: Lady's been shipped about.

DEBRIS: Sket ting!

SS VYPER: (Man already said she's nothing).

JONATHAN: Seen her crying in the ladies.

DEBRIS: Lady's men in line.

SS VYPER: She's a loo.

JONATHAN: Quick ting!

DEBRIS: (Man already said she's nothing).

SS VYPER: Touched once then –

ALL: Jezebel

13. Temple

DEBRIS: 2006, I'm sixteen.

HYPE: *The Guardian* gives Lethal B a column entitled 'David Cameron is a donut'. Astonishingly, Cameron shoots back with a whole article in the *Mail on Sunday* called 'You're talking rubbish, Lethal Bizzle'.

2006, DEBRIS is sixteen and discovering bashment. DJ plays dancehall mix showing the generations of dancehall feeding into grime.

It's the summer holidays before SS VYPER enters Year 13 and DEBRIS finishes secondary school, DEBRIS compels SS VYPER to stop revising and go to a shubz.

It's Elisa's sixteenth birthday, woi,
first shubz I've ever been to, boy,
batty-riders bestowed upon me, boy.
(Not entirely sure what a batty-rider is?)

But my friend came through, and lent me this,
it's a short, so short, gotta hide this –
burry batty-riders in recycling bin,
when the moon is full – we're going in.

SS VYPER concedes.

Change in the porch – parents sleeping,
drag Vyper on an N86,
top deck disciples gather on this,
passing round liquor like molasses.

Sony Ericsson against the glass: bliss,
amplifying beats into dark-ness,
night bus windows: mirrors,
– the plunge approaches.

And they levi-tate-a-bove their seats,
and their spines curve prophe-sies.
Gets dark as the inside-a me,
pelvis' fluid as a kettle's steam.

And they levi-tate-a-bove their seats,
and their spines curve prophe-sies.
Gets dark as the inside-a me,
pelvis' fluid as a kettle's steam.

When we get to the party we have to go in the back
entrance of this tiny hair salon which for some reason also
appears to sell children's bicycles? We walk in through the
back and it's RAMMED – I'm thinking about Mormon
young adult dances where my mum will literally go
around checking that any young people dancing with each
other are a Book of Mormon's width apart.

And the air is thick as the pink rum punch,
phone torches light limbs like stars,
following the riddim like a northern star.
Then like Moses, the ravers part.

And I start to move momentarily,
inspired by aunties' synchronicity,

but, then – become self-conscious…
(Have I got a front wedgy?)

SS VYPER: You okay D?

DEBRIS: I think so…

SS VYPER: Just let go…

DEBRIS: How you mean?

SS VYPER: I've never seen you just…let go, init? Everything
you're holding on to in there, just…let it go?

DEBRIS: And we levi-tate-a-bove our seats,
and our spines curve prophe-sies.
Gets dark as the inside-a me,
pelvis' fluid as a kettle's steam.

And we levi-tate-a-bove our seats,
and our spines curve prophe-sies.
Gets dark as the inside-a me,
pelvis' fluid as a kettle's steam.

Temple to temple, temple to temple,
temple to temple – a boy moves in,
renegade palm into my right hip,
other on waist as we breathe in sync.
This is what I'll learn we call whining.
– My body stops panicking –
something unlocked from this odd manikin,
look up at the ceiling it's raining,
look up at the ceiling it's raining,
look up at the ceiling it's raining,
so hot – condensation.

And I levi-tate-a-bove my seat,
and my spine curves prophe-sies.

Gets dark as the inside-a me,
pelvis fluid as a kettle's steam.

And I levi-tate-a-bove my seat,
and my spine curves prophe-sies.
Gets dark as the inside-a me,
pelvis fluid as a kettle's steam.

Mid-whine the speakers cut out and the lights go on – girls frantically try and fix their hair and make-up and mandem duck out of what was once an anonymous whine. DEBRIS looks up at the guy she was dancing with and awkwardly says 'hi' before running to find SS VYPER.

SS VYPER: For someone who's uncomfortable with a hug – I think you did pretty good at letting go just then.

DEBRIS: … What happened?

SS VYPER: Speakers cut out… Would you do it again?

DEBRIS: Yeah… I need to, I think…thank you.

'Candy' plays everyone runs back in, in rows for one last dance.

SS VYPER does the dance with everyone else in the party. DEBRIS doesn't know what to do… SS VYPER realizes and takes the time to teach it to her – mouthing instructions.

It takes a while – but she gets it – DEBRIS is in perfect sync with everyone else.

SS VYPER: You look mad pale, D.

DEBRIS vomits and passes out on the floor in a pile.

Shit. I get stopped by police for stopping fights. For fuck's sake D, how is getting caught with an unconscious white girl gunna go down?!

DEBRIS looks at SS VYPER and hugs him.

DEBRIS: I love you ya know, like really...like how ad libs love D Double E!

DEBRIS continues vomiting.

Spare keys –

SS VYPER rummages but the car alarm goes off. 'Sirens' by Dizzee Rascal intro of track.

SS VYPER: SHIT/SHIT/SHIT/SHIT/SHIT/SHIT/SHIT.

DEBRIS: Leave me in the porch!

SS VYPER: What?

DEBRIS: LEAVE!

'Sirens' by Dizzee Rascal continues – melodrama ensues. SS VYPER runs off but hides around a corner and waits to make sure DEBRIS gets in okay. DEBRIS is in the porch of her house unconscious.

DEBRIS: When I wake up, it's light outside, there is a glass of water on the toilet seat next to me. *Mum? Dad?* They've gone to church without me.

14. I Luv U: God Luvs U

MUM: Can I talk to you?

MUM takes a packet of cigarettes out of DEBRIS' blazer pocket.

Did Tony put you up to this?

DEBRIS: 'Cause I can't do anything for myself?

MUM: Deborah, you do know...

God loves you, God loves you, God loves you,
God loves you, God loves you, God loves you.

Is your brother really worth all this war?
You detour to him from God's front door!

Baptised at eight – consenting age – yes,
you swore – *unclean, Jesus' love, then pure.*

Eight's old enough to immerse body for.
I gave you life, what you bring battles for?

(I'm your saviour) my womb endured your toes like
blades to my ribs now more! Dad's all hush only knows
the hoover, Corry every evening, won't speak up.

Too poor for two so I work twenty-four and now I've hit
shore – for drug addiction galore?! Is it my fault –

Should I not work? Stay at home – let the bailiffs lurk?
Your brother's rhetoric forgets God's love. He's just an
anarchist shooting mud.

I begot you now beget God's dove.
Everything I taught you disposed of?

I've known you longer than you've known yourself,
Prophetess, know your wealth. Why

don't you have friends at church? Why
don't you thank me for birth?

DEBRIS: Did I ask to live, ya'kna? Ya scared of being alone,
ya past lives in this home,
and you've not outrun, what ya try'na explode –
Church is the pain we know.

MUM: Dad beat my mum with stick,
have you ever been hit?

Did we quit?
The devil is fit, the devil is legit and

46

these tools can
save you from it!

Are those your fags?

DEBRIS: Nah they ain't my fags!

MUM: But, I can smell fags?

DEBRIS: That kinda smell grabs!

MUM: Tell me the truth?

DEBRIS: I am!

MUM: Tell me the truth?

DEBRIS: I am!

MUM: Know God has a plan.

DEBRIS: What about my plan?

MUM: Listen to his plan.

DEBRIS: If I question plan?

MUM: You'll be left alone.

DEBRIS: I am!

MUM: In hell alone.

DEBRIS: I am.

> Your son's a rebel, I'm a maverick, don't be your dad – go
> on Catholic.
> Let's talk, let's ask, still Jew-ish, I want to tell you – I feel sick.
> If I did smoke, I'd talk, I'd sit – you repeat stick when I
> ain't done shit.

> Conflict: school, home (*deal with it*). God or you – who is
> strict?

You pick God, or your kids? You undermine where my
pain lives.
You just cry all manipulative; talk at me, don't let me give.
Hug me – don't see bully's bruises?

Friends vanish, into fists. Try to snitch, try to convict, told
teachers – but they fucked it.
Did I ask to live, ya'kna? Ya scared of being alone, ya past
lives in this home
and you've not outrun, what ya try'na explode – Church is
the pain we know.

MUM: I know where you were last night.

DEBRIS: I knew this wasn't about the fags…

MUM: I couldn't sleep, so when you didn't come home and I
found this…

MUM holds up DEBRIS' Sony Ericsson W810.

As a woman I found it offensive…. demeaning and
dangerous… I love you… please, stop this.

DEBRIS: That's mine… what are you doing?

MUM: This aggressive music… These lude dance moves
you're describing in here? It's wrong, Deborah. I love you,
and that's why I need to tell you, it's wrong. You know –

Dad beat my mum with stick,
have you ever been hit?

Did we quit?
The devil is fit, the devil is legit and

these tools can
save you from it!

So, are those your fags?

DEBRIS: Nah they ain't my fags!

MUM: But, I can smell fags?

DEBRIS: That kinda smell grabs!

MUM: Tell me the truth?

DEBRIS: I am!

MUM: Tell me the truth?

DEBRIS: I am!

MUM: Know God has a plan.

DEBRIS: What about my plan?

MUM: Listen to his plan.

DEBRIS: If I question plan?

MUM: You'll be left alone.

DEBRIS: I am!

MUM: In hell alone.

DEBRIS: I am…

> You know what, fuck it, they are my fags Mum, and I am done lying to you, living by your rules and being in this house!

15. Pretty Kemi's Perfect Pet

KEMI's house.

DEBRIS: Kemi is the Destiny's Child of our school; each thigh a Sunday roast, batty bursting denim, hair spiraling down her back like Turkey Twizzlers and her face doesn't need to try –

just a finger of Vaseline on her eyelids got Year 11's
rivalling.
I perch at the end of her bed, her pet rat nesting on her
shoulder,
she tells me not to be scared as its tail conducts the curls of
her hair –
it's so much softer than I expected, chunky and smooth as
a Babybel... She tells me, *closer* –
I run my hand down its body, feel its quiet undoing of
fear –
as my index finger slides into a full coil of Kemi's hair, we
laugh at how neatly
it fits as my knuckle kisses her ear and I remove my finger
slowly,
into her lap – she teaches me to roll, but I'm shit at it,
she places it soft between my lips like a secret but it is...
our secret, I think... Shit.

DEBRIS gets high for the first time and walks home.

It's 3am/I caress the door open into the dark living room/
Mum sits wide and waiting on the sofa/she looks up
at me/strokes the space next to her (despite my better
judgement) I sit. Maybe she knows...maybe she wants to
talk to me about it...maybe I could talk to her about it?
Maybe it would be okay? Maybe she would listen...

Yes, Mum?

MUM: I've noticed you've been going out a lot lately.

DEBRIS: I am sixteen now...

MUM: So, sometimes when you're going out are you...

DEBRIS: Am I...?

MUM: Going on...dates?

DEBRIS: Erm, yeah, I guess...sometimes they are, yeah.

MUM: Oh, okay, so sometimes are these dates with...erm... girls, with er, women, with females?

DEBRIS: Yes, Mum sometimes with females?

MUM: Oh I see, I see, I see, okay, so...erm... You, you, you, know how you've moved into Tony's old room?

DEBRIS: Yeah...?

MUM: Well... You must have noticed?

DEBRIS: What?

MUM: You remember when Tony was going wrong?

DEBRIS: Wrong? You mean when he was expelled from school for drug dealing?

MUM: Yes, well, when Tony was going wrong...when he lost his way...lost the word of God...fell foul to sin... Went wrong...

DEBRIS: Yeah I get it, Mum... Go on –

MUM: Well, at that time, Kat...

DEBRIS: (Kat is our cat, it's short for Katrina – I named her when I was ten) Kat?

MUM: Kat...she started... she started...crapping, outside of Tony's room.

DEBRIS: Right.

MUM: Well...

DEBRIS: Yes...?

MUM: She's started again.

DEBRIS: What?

MUM: Crapping.

DEBRIS: What?

MUM: Outside Tony's room.

DEBRIS: My room?

MUM: Your room now, yes.

DEBRIS: What?

MUM: I think she knows.

DEBRIS: Knows?

MUM: Knows you're going wrong.

DEBRIS: My mum thinks my cat is homophobic and sending messages from God via its arse! I can feel all the faith dropping out of me – like shit from a baby... Wrong yeah? Wrong? WE have been going wrong? Wrong. You know what, we have been going wrong actually, she's right, THIS is all wrong. Wrong, wrong, wrong. I'm always going to be wrong in this house and I need to find a way to make it right.

MUM: I think I should take your house keys till you've prayed about this properly.

DEBRIS: She corrals the house keys from my hand and FUCKING HUGS ME/I can't move/she doesn't notice/ I say nothing.

16. Goodbye

DEBRIS and SS VYPER sit at the top of the stairs of the Iron Bridge.

SS VYPER: We're two blacked-out bombers at the top of the Iron Bridge

DEBRIS: Chilling in jackets big as sleeping bags.

SS VYPER: Sippin' Strongbow blacks 'n' boost.

DEBRIS: We chat shit and smoke into the night sky –
I watch my own breath as it drifts into the fog lights.

SS VYPER: Over the trains and the estate.

BOTH: I can almost see my house from here.

SS VYPER: But not quite.

DEBRIS: I hope the other kids catch the ashes of our questions,
as we stub 'em out like shootin' stars,

SS VYPER: Rain 'n' police sirens.

*SS VYPER and DEBRIS stub out their cigarettes as they both exhale
their last draw. The sparks of the cigarettes can be seen under their
Air Force 1s.*

DEBRIS: V… Mum, God, School… I can't do it anymore.

SS VYPER: What?

DEBRIS: I don't want to leave YOU ya know. You're the only
thing here for me.

SS VYPER: Yeah, I know.

DEBRIS: What you gunna do…

SS VYPER: Cry into your empty blazer?

DEBRIS: Fuck off… I mean you're nearly in Year 13…we've
both dreamt of leaving.

SS VYPER: I always know what you MEAN, you know.

DEBRIS: Remember what you told me the other day.

SS VYPER: Don't trust men that wear white shoes –

DEBRIS: V!… You said, let go…just let go init.

SS VYPER: 'Cause dat ended so well?

DEBRIS: Yo, I had fun… Can't you just let go?

SS VYPER: We don't all have that luxury… I got to think about who I'd be dropping.

SS VYPER and DEBRIS hug.

DEBRIS: That was the first time I think I let anyone properly hug me.

Going on Monday V.

SS VYPER: Oh.

DEBRIS: It's only one train to Chelmsford, I forged Mum's signature on some documents, I'm moving out into some sheltered B&B ting for kids who've been kicked out.

SS VYPER: Shit.

BOTH: Shit-den.

SS VYPER and DEBRIS tag their fists together then walk separate ways off the bridge.

This is the last time DEBRIS and SS VYPER see each other for twelve years.

17. 12 Years Of Grime

SS VYPER: That was twelve years ago, what have you been up to since?

2007, grime audio clips about why grime isn't dead.

DJ: 2007, Logan Sama provokes the scene by saying that grime is dead. Wiley says, 'It takes 10, 15, 20 years to build a scene. Don't worry, grime ain't dead just give it the same time hip hop and rock have had to flourish.'

DEBRIS: I'm scouted by Channel 4 and they follow my journey as a young post-Mormon dyslexic trying to become a poet.

SS VYPER: All the youngers keep coming to me just to show me their bars. I'm reluctant at first but eventually I decide to spend the summer mentoring a few kids from the estate who've got potential.

2008, 'Wearing My Rolex' by Wiley mixed with 'Dance wiv Me' by Dizzee Rascal featuring Calvin Harris.

DJ: 2008, the charge for chart success from grime artists begins. Underground grime artists are emerging on to the same platforms as artists like Calvin Harris and Rihanna.

DEBRIS: I get my first paid writing commission from Louis Vuitton and perform at the opening of their store on New Bond Street in front of Bob Geldof, Jude Saw and Elle Macpherson.

SS VYPER: I get 86% in my first year of uni, a couple of the MCs I'm recording start getting their tracks on channel U.

2009, 'Too Many Man' by Boy Better Know grime mixed with Brap Pack soundbite.

DJ: 2009, form 696 shuts down all the grime raves, leaving me out of a job and killing one of the key monetizing avenues for grime at the time. Once again – black entrepreneurship is criminalized.

2010, 'Pass Out' by Tinie Tempah mixed with 'Street Fighter Riddim' by D Double E mixed. News clips from uni riots.

2011, audio clips from UK-wide riots.

DJ: 2001, UK riots are sparked over the murder of Mark Duggan. Disorder continues to blight the country for six days, with *The Guardian* naming 'Pow' the 'anthem for the kettled youth'. Whatever the real reason for the rioting, it's clear – from the roads to the music – we can't be ignored anymore.

2012, 'Ill Manors' by Plan B mixed with London Olympic performance by Dizzee Rascal.

DJ: 2012, local businesses are displaced, and council estates are to make space for the London 2012 Olympics in Stratford (where there is a ten year waiting list for a two bedroom council house). Dizzee performs 'Bonkers' at the Olympic Opening Ceremony, but lives in the US.

SS VYPER: An old video of me spitting goes viral, I start getting calls to make tunes... I even write one. But then I decide the traction could be better used elsewhere, you know? I set up a studio at the uni campus in Stratford and start bringing MCs there.

2014, 'German Whip' by Meridian Dan ft Big H & JME.

DJ: 2014, Kanye West brings out Jammer, Skepta, Shorty, Krept, Konan, Novelist, Stormzy and Fekky at the Brit Awards. Meanwhile, underground a new generation of MCs begin to revive the pirate radio circuit.

2015, 'Shut Up' by Stormzy mixed with 'Shut Down' by Skepta.

2015, for the first time ever, Dizzee Rascal performs the entirety of *Boy in da Corner* in New York – there is an international appetite for grime music.

DEBRIS: I'm invited to Buckingham Palace to meet the Queen because of my work as a poet.

SS VYPER: The youts on the estate get a hold of an old video of me spitting and won't leave me alone about it until SBTV approach me to do a new school F64 for YouTube.

2016, 'Queen's Speech 4' by Lady Leshurr, 2016 mixed into Skepta's Mercury award acceptance speech.

DJ: 2016, grime journalist, Hyperfrank, petitions to bring Dizzee's *Boy in da Corner* performance to the UK and finally it comes home to East London the same year Skepta wins the mercury prize for *Konnichiwa.*

DEBRIS: I find that kid amongst the bins outside my house in Nottingham.

SS VYPER: For some mad reason my F64 goes viral. All of a sudden I've signed up to Twitter and I have... Supporters... Mad init? Guess I'm an MC again?

2017, mix of political references from grime tracks and interview between JME and Jeremy Corbyn.

DJ: 2017, grime not only sells units but changes policies. Form 696 gets scrapped because a body of research by Westminster University and Ticketmaster proves it is an economy so big the government cannot justify shutting it down.

DEBRIS: I go to a seminar about working with young people who have suffered trauma and I'm told that the key difference between someone who can and cannot overcome their trauma is having one person who understands you. That person for me Vyper, was you... but I couldn't find your number...

SS VYPER: So you couldn't type my name into Facebook or Twitter?

DEBRIS: I didn't think –

SS VYPER: Sounds like it.

DEBRIS: ...

SS VYPER: Do you know his name?

DEBRIS: Whose?

SS VYPER: The kid you used my bars to 'save'?

DEBRIS: No…

SS VYPER: What a surprise…

DEBRIS: I decided to move back here so…

SS VYPER: Abandoning people's a habit, yeah?

DEBRIS: Wow. Okay, yeah… Giving up my career, my home, and my adult life to live with my crazy Mormon parents in a shoebox room at twenty-eight…yeah, I ditched everyone in Notts to live the dream!

SS VYPER: But you did abandon ME to live the dream it seems?

DEBRIS: It wasn't just you, I haven't even talked to Tony yet – it's all reminders of stuff I couldn't handle. I think that's why I was constantly addressing it as anecdote…story, poem.

SS VYPER: Wouldn't be the first time I've been a white girl's inspiring anecdote…

DEBRIS: Yeah, I guess I deserve that.

SS VYPER: And what do you GUESS I deserve?

DEBRIS: I'm sorry…

SS VYPER: …?

DEBRIS: I ran away –

SS VYPER: I couldn't –

DEBRIS: Take it anymore –

SS VYPER: If I didn't take it, my mum would, and I wasn't gonna have that.

DEBRIS: Going home was too hard.

SS VYPER: Home is too hard…for me to leave the people I
love to it…

DEBRIS: … Stop.

SS VYPER: All this justification, but I still don't understand
why you are chatting ABOUT ME yet still not chatting
TO ME –

18. The Clash

DEBRIS: So why didn't I invite you?
Had to return to mum before I returned to you.
Had to unpack my truth before I came to you.
Being honest to me, before I'm honest to you.

Saving other people 'cause I couldn't save you.
Tried to take responsibility with privilege too.
But I ran away from me when I ran away from you.
Lugging pack lunches in my backpack too.

Don't forget I was a waitress at uni too,
organizing festivals for free too,
covering train fair – from – too –
porridge and water for a term or two.

I ain't saying – I worked harder than you.
Fucked up – luck's got a colour, true.
That's why I'm making work like this –
ask the audience – why am I here not you?

SS VYPER: I can't rate that that's not
right…how can you take something we
do on a day to day then go and change your
life; meanwhile V's nowhere in
sight; I won't draw for the race card that's

fine; but same time I ain't gunna sit here and lie; me and
you both started the same
way but you had things easier cos you're

white; don't get it twisted – I'm not this
missing your personal struggle but that's just life; but you
and I ain't fighting the same
fight; as a matter of fact it don't com-
pare when you see violence from all
sides; you just fight with your mother and
cry; I could have a fight in the street and die.

DEBRIS: You trying to publicly shame me?
Like you don't even know me? Like I wasn't grafting from
pre-sixteen –
building this pathway brick by brick.

Writing every day – Bic by Bic.
Not just poems but funding bids.
Not just for me – nuff man in the bitz. Wasn't easy to
adapt to this business –

Working in a theatre – real shoes, shit.
In academia – dyslexic,
Lecturers assuming dat I'm stupid, students assuming I'm
another student.

But I never questioned this – same gift gifted from
unraveled fist –
Other kids in corners needing this.
Should I ignore or use privilege?

SS VYPER: I hear you, but it don't make no
difference; none of what you said makes your fight
equivalent; you're just standing here;
appropriating our culture and acting

innocent; either that or you're choosing
ignorance; nobody here's done their due
diligence; otherwise everybody would have been
calling you out for silencing my ex-

perience; cos you say that you're
helping – but how does it help us?
You're up here quoting my old
bars and I'm still up in the ends no changes; tried helping
some of my old
friends but I just see pain in faces;
I faced up to my
realities you ran too far away places; that explains it...

DEBRIS: What? I didn't steal your shit?
I mentioned your name before I said it.
In the literary world it's called a credit,
if you wanna learn the craft you got to mimic.

Or should there be no grime show?
When they had asked me, should I have said no?
When people ask me should I not say so –
How did you get here? Who do you know?

Redistribute this shit – one locked room – all the resources
When they let me in should I'a ran from this?
Or stash and grab redistribute this?

I had a once suicidal student
start their own business,
teenagers once homeless
getting A*'s in English.

SS VYPER: Let's be real no need for pre-
tending, if I don't like what I'm seeing I'm
sending; equally, that doesn't mean it was

easy for you being gay or Dyslexic – I ain't gunna tell you nobody
gets it; I ain't gunna tell you we don't respect it, but for you to stand there and
tell me our struggles the same is somewhat per-

plexing; I ain't gunna lie that's mad that's a
next ting; something's wrong here it needs co-
rrecting; If you were a black girl doing this
show there's no way you coulda been out here
flexing; organisations must love
wheeling you out when they want a new cash in-
jection, this some new age blaxploi-
tation but this generation won't ac-
cept it –

DEBRIS: Yes, I fucked up –
When I had to leave with all my stuff.
Yes, I fucked up –
I abandoned you then I called it love.

Yes, I fucked up –
Glamorized your plight – not doing enough.
I fucked up, I fucked up.
I'm sorry – it's not enough.

SS VYPER: Nah, nah; where's my
P; this is my story – where's my
P; can't rate that you're out here and there's
old friends sitting in jail like where's my P?

These are my bars; where's my
P; this is my story – where's my
P; even made me pay to sit
here just so I can ask you where's my
P?

DEBRIS: I was a coward because I boxed up my trauma and
   left it behind in that house and in doing so, I couldn't turn
   back –

Intro of 'Do it' by Dizzee Rascal.

19. Going Home

DEBRIS: Mum is delicate; a Quentin Blake illustration,
   an adult through a kaleidoscope, struggling with the porch
   front-door handle (still broken, the same white plastic
   frame) she's in stop motion,
   (I imagine her) trapped in a giant piece of Tupperware –
   fraught.

MUM: When you didn't call, or answer or come home – I prayed.
   For years I prayed and prayed and prayed.

DEBRIS: Mum, I know church may have saved you from your
   trauma but you know, it was ours…

MUM: I know… I'm sorry.

DEBRIS: Mum goes to hug me and I flinch and she sees me
   (finally) and stops herself.

   *'Do It' by Dizzee Rascal comes back in and gets louder towards the
   end of the song.*

   I put my hand on her shoulder – thank you.

   I'm done packing up and passing it on,
   it was only when I put my hand on my mum's shoulder
   that this packed lunch backpack was gone.

   MUM disappears, and DEBRIS turns to SS VYPER.

   Could we maybe start this again…the right way?

SS VYPER: Aye?

DEBRIS: Got a USB on your key chain?

20. Way Back

SS VYPER chucks his USB to the DJ and chats to her about the show.
HYPE and DEBRIS do shout outs to people in the audience that have
been involved in the show. Audience members possibly invited on stage.

DJ: Yes

You're locked into the I Am Grime show.

Hold on, I think we have a caller.

Wah gwan, caller? What have you got to say?

SS VYPER: Yeah, wah gwan? Like, obviously

I'm listening to your show uh huh

And like, a lot of these guys, they don't know about grime,
like (yeah)

They know about grime now but they don't know about
grime alright before it was grime but it weren't called
garage, you get me?

And man are talking like they know history (you're
schooling 'em)

Man don't know history, fam (alright, alright, alright)

Obviously these MCs think grime started with 'Pow!'

DJ: Alright, do your ting, boss.

SS VYPER: Alright, cool.

I started in 2002

Locked onto Deja, bars on the paper

Way before Kano was a big baider

Before Terror Danjah made 'Radar'

Way back when I had Air Max trainers

I was in school, doing sets with Vader
And I never done work in class
I just spat bars till I needed an inhaler
I 'member Deja on a Monday night
I used to turn into the radio taper
Saturday night was an East Coast ting
I used to rate Demon and Maxo Ranger
So they can't tell me I don't know about grime
I be like rudeboy, nuh mek me get serious
My dad was a music man
Mum was a UKG raver

'Cause I've been on it since the wickedest ting
Way before Tinch said 'back, you know'
Them times Wiley said 'Tiger, Tiger'
Now I'm gonna kill 'em with the new school flow
I never used to roll deep regular
I stayed in to listen to the radio shows
Then I heard Esco say 'man are murderer'
Then I knew that grime had evolved

Remember when Jme first got known
I heard him and Big H on the radio
Way before Chipmunk ever said sho
Meridian came before Boy Better Know
I was at home, hearing about raves
These times, I was too young to go to the shows
I wanted to go, yeah, man, standing just to hear
'5000 volts, it's your own fault'
Whoa, these youts, what do they know?
They just wanna do grime for the payload
But you can't be a vet if you think that 'Ps & Qs'

Is the first tune by Kano
Uneducated youts better lay low
Think they can get by with the same flow
They wanna search for all the money in grime
But won't find nothing after the rainbow

'Cause I've been on it since the wickedest ting
Way before Tinch said 'back, you know'
Them times Wiley said 'Tiger, Tiger'
Now I'm gonna kill 'em with the new school flow
I never used to roll deep regular
I stayed in to listen to the radio shows
Then I heard Esco say 'man are murderer'
Then I knew that grime had evolved

'Cause I've been on it since the wickedest ting
Way before Tinch said 'back, you know'
Them times Wiley said 'Tiger, Tiger'
Now I'm gonna kill 'em with the new school flow
I never used to roll deep regular
I stayed in to listen to the radio shows
Then I heard Esco say 'man are murderer'
Then I knew that grime had evolved

Look, so when you hear this
Better keep calm and just play the garage
First heard house at like '98
Since then, it's been the longest marriage
I don't wanna hear no talk about novice
I've been on this ting since Mystic and Manic
Way before Willy and Diz stopped talking
And the whole scene used to rave in Palace

Yo, so when you hear this
Better keep calm and just play the garage
First heard house at like '98
Ever since, it's been the longest marriage
I don't wanna hear no talk about novice
I was on this ting since Mystic and Manic
Way before Willy and Diz stopped talking
And the whole scene used to rave in Palace

With the badboy style
Hit them with the 1s and 2
With the ba-ba-ba-ba-badboy style
With the raving crew
History lesson
For the day
I'm k-k-k-k-doin' it again
Yeah, it's a vibe, yo
With the, with the raving
With the raving crew
With the 1, 2, hit 'em with the raving crew
Enter, enter
Enter
Yo
Ooh, ooh, ooh, ooh, ooh
It's all fun, man
There's no more fun in grime no more
Everyone's on this
Screw man and box man in the face ting
Dead that, man

The END.

WWW.OBERONBOOKS.COM